TELEPHONES

Words over Wires

These and other books are included in the
Encyclopedia of Discovery and Invention series:

Airplanes

Anesthetics

Animation

Atoms

Clocks

Computers

Genetics

Germs

Gravity

Human Origins

Lasers

Microscopes

Movies

Phonograph

Photography

Plate Tectonics

Printing Press

Radar

Railroads

Ships

Telephones

Telescopes

Television

Vaccines

TELEPHONES
Words over Wires

by MARCUS WEBB

■ ■

The ENCYCLOPEDIA of
D·I·S·C·O·V·E·R·Y
and INVENTION

P.O. Box 289011 SAN DIEGO, CA 92198-9011

Printed in the U.S.A.

Library of Congress Cataloging-in-Publication Data

Webb, Marcus, 1957-
  Telephones, words over wires / by Marcus Webb.

    p. cm.—(The Encyclopedia of discovery and invention)
  Includes bibliographical references and index.
    Summary: Discusses the invention of the telephone and
technological advances and future developments in
telephone equipment and services.
    ISBN 1-56006-219-3
    1. Telephone—Juvenile literature.   [1. Telephone.]
I. Title.   II. Series.
TK6165.W43 1992   92-11400
                                                    CIP
                                                     AC

Contents

■■■

Foreword

The belief in progress has been one of the dominant forces in Western Civilization from the Scientific Revolution of the seventeenth century to the present. Embodied in the idea of progress is the conviction that each generation will be better off than the one that preceded it. Eventually, all peoples will benefit from and share in this better world. R.R. Palmer, in his *History of the Modern World,* calls this belief in progress "a kind of nonreligious faith that the conditions of human life" will continually improve as time goes on.

For over a thousand years prior to the seventeenth century, science had progressed little. Inquiry was largely discouraged, and experimentation, almost nonexistent. As a result, science became regressive and discovery was ignored. Benjamin Farrington, a historian of science, characterized it this way: "Science had failed to become a real force in the life of society. Instead there had arisen a conception of science as a cycle of liberal studies for a privileged minority. Science ceased to be a means of transforming the conditions of life." In short, had this intellectual climate continued, humanity's future would have been little more than a clone of its past.

Fortunately, these circumstances were not destined to last. By the seventeenth and eighteenth centuries, Western society was undergoing radical and favorable changes. And the changes that occurred gave rise to the notion that progress was a real force urging civilization forward. Surpluses of consumer goods were replacing substandard living conditions in most of Western Europe. Rigid class systems were giving way to social mobility. In nations like France and the United States, the lofty principles of democracy and popular sovereignty were being painted in broad, gilded strokes over the fading canvasses of monarchy and despotism.

But more significant than these social, economic, and political changes, the new age witnessed a rebirth of science. Centuries of scientific stagnation began crumbling before a spirit of scientific inquiry that spawned undreamed of technological advances. And it was the discoveries and inventions of scores of men and women that fueled these new technologies, dramatically increasing the ability of humankind to control nature—and, many believed, eventually to guide it.

It is a truism of science and technology that the results derived from observation and experimentation are not finalities. They are part of a process. Each discovery is but one piece in a continuum bridging past and present and heralding an extraordinary future. The heroic age of the Scientific Revolution was simply a start. It laid a foundation upon which succeeding generations of imaginative thinkers could build. It kindled the belief that progress is possible as long as there were gifted men and women who would respond to society's needs. When Antonie van Leeuwenhoek observed *Animalcules* (little animals) through his high-powered microscope in 1683, the discovery did not end there. Others followed who would call these "little animals" bacteria and, in time, recognize their role in the process of health and disease. Robert Koch, a German bacteriologist and winner of the Nobel Prize in Physiology and Medicine, was one of these men. Koch firmly established that bacteria are responsible for causing infectious diseases. He identified, among others, the causative organisms of anthrax and tuberculosis. Alexander Fleming, another Nobel Laureate, progressed still further in the quest to understand and control bacteria. In 1928, Fleming discovered penicillin, the antibiotic wonder drug. Penicillin, and the generations of antibiotics that succeeded it, have done more to

prevent premature death than any other discovery in the history of humankind. And as civilization hastens toward the twenty-first century, most agree that the conquest of van Leeuwenhoek's "little animals" will continue.

The *Encyclopedia of Discovery and Invention* examines those discoveries and inventions that have had a sweeping impact on life and thought in the modern world. Each book explores the ideas that led to the invention or discovery, and, more importantly, how the world changed and continues to change because of it. The series also highlights the people behind the achievements—the unique men and women whose singular genius and rich imagination have altered the lives of everyone. Enhanced by photographs and clearly explained technical drawings, these books are comprehensive examinations of the building blocks of human progress.

TELEPHONES

Words over Wires

TELEPHONES

Introduction

The telephone and what it represents—instant communication over long distances—is so common today that people hardly think of the telephone as a machine. Yet the telephone represents the climax of many generations of effort, learning, and ambition.

Today this tool allows people around the world to speak directly to each other and to hear each other's voices at the exact moment their words are spoken. The telephone has made communication as swift as thought and as intimate as a whisper. In the words of Thomas Edison, who helped improve the early telephone, Alexander Graham Bell's invention erased "time and space and brought the human family closer together."

The telephone is also the key instrument in an ongoing electronic communications revolution that is changing civilization. For centuries before the telephone, the printed word was the most important method of communication.

Today the telephone has almost completely replaced the private letters and individual messengers that were used as recently as the early 1900s. Bolstered by the telephone, electronic me-

... TIMELINE: **TELEPHONES**

1 >   2 > 3 > 4 > 5 > 6 >   7 >

1 ■ 1844
An electric telegraph transmits the first instant long-distance message in the United States.

2 ■ 1876
American inventor Alexander Graham Bell perfects the first working model of a telephone.

3 ■ 1877
The Bell Telephone Company sells the first commercial telephones.

4 ■ 1878
The first central exchanges begin operation.

5 ■ 1885
Bell Telephone forms a subsidiary, American Telephone & Telegraph (AT&T), to create a national long-distance network.

6 ■ 1892
The first long-distance service connects New York and Chicago.

7 ■ 1915
The first coast-to-coast telephone conversation takes place.

8 ■ 1927
Regular commercial telephone service between New York and London begins.

9 ■ 1935
American Bell stages the first around-the-world telephone call.

dia, such as radio, movies, and television, have become more powerful than newspapers and magazines. Linked by the telephone, computers and other new electronic media are challenging the place of books and libraries.

Unlike print, the telephone makes sounds that people can hear, whether they listen closely or not. How something is said—the tone of voice, the accompanying laughter, or a catch in the throat—is at least as important as the words that are spoken. The words, sounds, and emotional overtones sent over the telephone are grasped instantly, not slowly, the way a written message is. Also, as with many later elec-

tronic media, the telephone brings a form of communication that appeals to the emotions.

More and more, we live in a world of instant sounds, live images, simultaneous transmissions, and worldwide access. It is a world born of the telephone, a world shaped by the telephone, and a world still changing because of the telephone. As new technologies appear in the future, these too will be adapted to work with the telephone. The humble telephone, almost forgotten as the basis of the modern communications revolution, will continue to serve as humanity's electronic central nervous system.

8 > 9 > 10> 11> 12>13> 14> 15> 16>

10 ■ 1942
The army links the continental United States to the Territory of Alaska by telephone cable.

11 ■ 1947
Three scientists at Bell Labs invent the transistor.

12 ■ 1962
AT&T creates, and the National Aeronautics and Space Administration launches, the first two-way communications satellite.

13 ■ 1965
The first electronic switching station begins active service. Commercial telephone service using satellites to link the United States and Europe begins.

14 ■ 1980
The first 900-number, pay-per-minute, telephone calls are introduced.

15 ■ 1984
As the result of a government lawsuit, AT&T agrees to end its monopoly over the telephone industry.

16 ■ 1991
Soviet citizens use telephone fax machines to tell the world about an attempted government coup.

The Story of Instant Communication

Before the invention of the telephone and other modern communication devices, the idea of sending a message instantly across vast distances seemed magical and mysterious. People considered such communication impossible. Only a supernatural being like Mercury, the mythological messenger to the Roman gods, could accomplish instant long-distance communication.

The Romans said that whenever the king of the gods wished to communicate anywhere in the universe, he sent Mercury. In a flash Mercury would appear someplace else and deliver the message. People liked the idea of Mer-

Mercury, the Roman messenger of the gods, instantly carried messages over great distances.

cury because they wished to be able to perform instant long-distance communication themselves, but they did not know how. The history of the telephone is the story of how human beings achieved the power to do something that was once considered godlike.

The Need for Rapid Communication

People have always needed to send and receive messages quickly to distant places. Fast and accurate communication could make the difference between victory and defeat, between profit and loss, even between life and death. In early societies one village might need to warn its neighbors of oncoming danger, about visitors or strangers in the area, or ask for emergency help or medical information in cases of disaster, injury, or illness.

As societies became more complex, the need for rapid long-distance communication became even greater. Friendly armies that were physically far apart needed to tell each other what the enemy was doing. The allies wanted to coordinate their tactics quickly, before the enemy acted. Merchants needed to send and receive the latest information about what goods were wanted, where, and at what price. They could then buy or sell items that were still available or in demand.

Before the age of electricity, people

American Indians communicated over long distances using smoke signals.

sent messages as quickly as they knew how: at the speed of a runner, horse, drum relay, or other signals. Thousands of years ago, the people of the Congo, in Africa, sent messages from village to village by using tom-toms, or "talking drums." These drums imitated the high and low sounds of the drummers' language, and they could be heard miles away.

Another early example of rapid long-distance communication was the use of smoke signals by American Indians. A messenger built a fire, then held or released large and small puffs of smoke. Different combinations of smoke puffs had different meanings. Three small puffs might have warned of danger, for example.

Rapid long-distance communication was accomplished at sea with flag signals. This system, created more than two thousand years ago by Greek and Phoenician sailors, used many different flags to relay messages. For example, a green flag might have meant "land is nearby."

Centuries later, naval flag communications developed into the semaphore system, which used only two flags held in a sailor's hands. Different positions of the two flags symbolized different letters. Holding both flags down and to the right, for example, represented the letter *A.*

The semaphore system proved so flexible and efficient at sea that a French engineer named Claude Chappe adapted it for use on land in the late 1700s. Chappe did this for the French government so that politicians and military men could send their messages quickly. He built a series of towers on hilltops that could be seen from five miles away. These towers were narrow, tall buildings, with movable wooden arms. Different positions of the arms symbolized different letters, just as different positions of the semaphore flags had done at sea.

Claude Chappe's hundreds of signal towers relayed messages in minutes across the French countryside.

By building hundreds of towers across the countryside, Chappe created a relay system that could send a message five hundred miles in fifteen minutes. That was much faster than sending a message by horse, which would usually take at least a day to go the same distance. It could mean the difference between surprise or readiness in battle, victory or defeat in war.

Chappe's relay system was called a telegraph from two ancient Greek words: *tele*, meaning "distant," and *graph*, meaning "writing." A telegraph, then, was a "distant-writing" communications system.

This method of communication was fast, but not instant. Instant communication did not become possible until people learned how to control and use one of the basic forms of energy in the universe, electricity.

Batteries, Wires, and Magnets

Today people know many things about electricity. They know that electricity moves at the speed of light. They know how to create, store, control, and use electricity as a power source for machines. Only two centuries ago, however, nobody knew any of this. Gradually, as people learned how electricity works, they also realized it could become a tool for instant communication—first with the electric telegraph, then with the telephone.

In 1800 an Italian scientist named Alessandro Volta invented the first battery. This battery provided a controllable supply of direct current, or steady impulses of electricity. In 1820 a Danish physicist named Hans Oersted was try-

The battery invented by Alessandro Volta gave other inventors an important tool for controlling electric current.

ing to discover how electricity works. He found that he could send electricity through a short wire that he coiled around a compass needle. When the electrical impulses flowed through the coil, the compass needle moved. The experiment showed that electricity and magnetism were somehow connected and that electricity could control magnets.

Amateur and professional scientists everywhere realized what this might mean. Perhaps electricity moving through wires could be used to stop and start magnetic activity at some distant point on the far end of the wire. The challenge lay in controlling the current so that it flowed in set patterns. These patterns of flowing current would cause a needle or pencil at the other end to move. The needle would point to specific letters of the alphabet, depending on the pattern or burst of current. The pencil would mark a piece of paper with a symbol that represented a letter of the alphabet. The complete system of electrical impulses creating magnetic-based alphabetic signals would be known as an electric telegraph. At last messages could be sent instantly over a long distance.

As a result, communication would become much faster, more precise, and far more reliable. Lives could be saved, wars could be won, fortunes could be built, criminals could be caught, and civilization could be spread through a reliable system of instant communication. All of this, and more, was to happen with the invention of the electric telegraph and, later, the telephone. First, though, a great deal of work remained.

Over the next several years, scientists in Europe and America tried many experiments to see if a real electric tele-graph could be built. An American professor and physicist named Joseph Henry created a practical, working version of an electric telegraph in 1831. He strung a mile of wire around his classroom and put a battery and transmitter on one end of the wire. (A transmitter is something that could turn on and off the connection between the wire and battery.) Henry wrapped the other end of the wire around an iron bar.

When Henry sent current from the battery through the wire, it magnetized the iron bar, creating an electromagnet. Next to the electromagnet was a permanent magnet—a piece of metal, like a compass needle, that is always magnetic, even without electricity to help it. The permanent magnet was attracted to the electromagnet, and it swung toward the electromagnet and rang a small bell. This provided an audio signal that Henry hoped could be the basis for an electric telegraph code. Henry's work laid the foundation for a commercial telegraph system. Unfortunately, fame and fortune went to those who came after him.

Joseph Henry thrilled onlookers with his successful demonstration of an electric telegraph. The demonstration showed that electricity and magnetism were the keys to instant, long-distance communication.

In 1832, the year after Henry's experiment, a Boston doctor named Charles Jackson made an ocean voyage from Paris to the United States. To amuse his shipmates, Jackson demonstrated how electricity going through wire that was wrapped around a horseshoe could magnetize the metal and attract nails. Jackson explained to his fellow passengers that electricity could be sent over a wire for many miles.

Jackson did not grasp the full significance of this, however. He viewed his demonstration as simple amusement. "A pretty scientific toy, isn't it?" Jackson asked. "But it's not likely to be of much practical use."

Samuel Morse's Telegraph

One of the passengers who saw the demonstration was a forty-year-old American painter named Samuel Morse. Like many painters, Morse was in constant need of money. He had been experimenting with electricity for ten years, hoping to invent something profitable enough to free him to paint in peace.

Jackson's demonstration was nothing new, but Morse was inspired by it. "If the presence of electricity can be made visible in any part of an electrical circuit [that is] closed by an electro-magnet," Morse wrote, "I see no reason why intelligence [information] may not be transmitted instantaneously by electricity."

During the remainder of his ocean voyage, Morse worked out a system for an electric telegraph. He planned to use bursts of electricity to activate the magnet and cause a pencil in the receiving instrument to make zigzag lines on paper. The zigzag lines would form a sort of written semaphore code, based on the U.S. Navy's flag system.

Practical considerations, like earning a living, forced Morse to postpone work on his telegraph idea. Within about two years, though, Morse was earning enough money from a college teaching job to resume his research. He rented a small room to use as a laboratory and built crude models. One was made by using machinery from inside a clock to move a paper roll. In this way lengthy signals could be continuously recorded on blank paper.

Morse's pen-and-paper recording device worked well enough, but his telegraph faced a major problem: resistance. Electricity resists going through a wire; the farther it goes, the weaker it gets. Eventually, if a person tries to send electricity through a long enough wire, the current dies out altogether, and nothing much happens at the other end. No message would get through.

Samuel Morse saw great potential in an electric telegraph system. His system would rely on bursts of electricity and a written code.

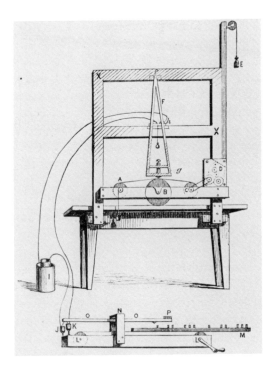

Morse's first telegraph was built by mechanic Alfred Vail and was tested at Boston City College in 1837.

The code of zigzag lines said "Successful experiment with telegraph, Sept. 4, 1837." Morse was happy with his results but decided he could create a more efficient code based on a simpler writing system. A combination of dots and dashes would represent each letter. These signals could easily be sent with long and short bursts of electricity and would be easier to read on the receiving end. This system came to be known as Morse code, and is still in use today.

Early Application of the Telegraph

That same year, 1837, two English scientists named William Cooke and Charles Wheatstone created a five-needle telegraph. This telegraph used a much more complex code system that was based on different needle positions to represent different letters. When they sent a message, no written record was created, but their five-needle telegraph worked. Telegraph lines were installed

Making a practical, usable telegraph meant that Morse had to find some way to strengthen the signal as it passed through long wires.

Morse did this by inventing an electrical relay to send the message along in stages. He simply placed batteries partway along the wire, and they added strength to each burst of electricity that came along. The result was a strong signal that could jump through the wire from battery to battery and finally arrive very far away.

Morse was no craftsman, however. To build a better model of his telegraph, he hired a mechanic named Alfred Vail. When it was completed, Morse and Vail set up their improved device in a lecture hall at Boston's City College. It worked! The very first telegram was transmitted from one corner of the hall to another.

Morse's simple, efficient telegraph code consists of a series of dots and dashes representing letters, numbers, and punctuation marks.

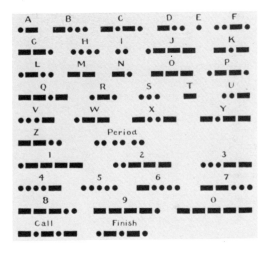

alongside British railway tracks, and routine traffic messages began crackling between stations, faster than the trains themselves.

Back in America, Samuel Morse successfully demonstrated his telegraph to the U.S. Congress and asked for thirty thousand dollars to set up an experimental telegraph line. The money was hard to get. Many congressmen thought delivery of mail by train, ship, and horse was a good enough means of communication. They did not want to waste thirty-thousand dollars of the taxpayers' money on any newfangled, unnecessary inventions.

Some leaders did realize how vital improved communications could be. Perhaps they remembered that Andrew Jackson's soldiers had fought the Battle of New Orleans in 1815, only because horseback messengers arrived too late with the news that the war with Britain was over. Political and commercial uses for instant communication were also obvious to these congressmen. A country with interests from Maine to California could not afford to send messages at the speed of a horse! After years of delay and debate, Congress finally voted to spend the thirty thousand dollars to construct a telegraph line between Washington, D.C., and Baltimore, Maryland.

Telegraph wires were strung on a series of twenty-four-foot-tall wooden poles, which were erected alongside the Baltimore-Washington railroad tracks. On May 24, 1844, Morse sat down at the

Bursts of electricity activated a pencil on Morse's telegraph. The pencil recorded dots and dashes along a moving paper ribbon.

MORSE'S TELEGRAPH KEY

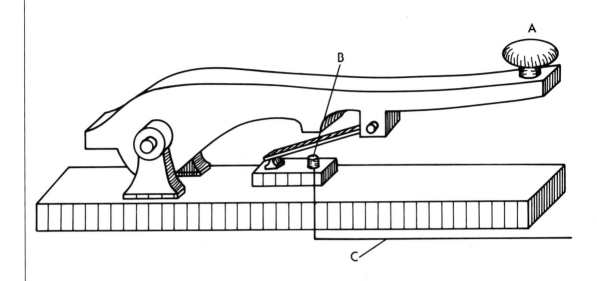

A telegraph key is a switch that turns an electrical circuit on and off, allowing an operator to send a message by wire. When the operator depresses the key (A), an electrical connection is made (B). This connection sends an electrical impulse along a transmission wire (C) to a receiving telegraph station. When the operator releases the key, the connection breaks and the flow of the electrical impulses stops. By repeatedly tapping the key and releasing it, the operator can control the impulses sent over the wires. These controlled impulses form a coded series of short and long signals representing numbers, letters, and punctuation marks.

transmitter in the U.S. Supreme Court, then located in a chamber of the Capitol building. He used his code of short and long bursts to send the first official telegraph message to his partner, Alfred Vail, at the receiving station in Baltimore.

The message Morse sent was suggested by Annie Ellsworth, daughter of the patents commissioner. It was a quotation from the Bible: "What hath God wrought!" This religious expression of awe showed just how revolutionary the electric telegraph really was. Morse's message traveled at the speed of electricity, which means it traveled at the speed of light itself. On that day, human beings sent a message over a great distance as quickly as could ever be carried by the mythological messenger, Mercury. A new era in human communication had begun.

At first, few people realized the importance of this new invention. In fact, most people did not understand anything about electricity and could not

(Left) Actors recreate the moment when Morse sent the first telegraph message, "What hath God wrought!" (Below) The first telegraph line went up between Washington, D.C. and Baltimore, Maryland, only after years of congressional debate.

believe that Morse's system actually worked. But events quickly proved the true power of the telegraph.

In 1844, two days after Morse sent that first message, he and Vail telegraphed news about the Democratic party convention in Baltimore back and forth between Congress and the party delegates. The politicians were stunned to realize that the telegraph's instant news, sent over a magical electric wire, was just as accurate as that of an official party messenger who arrived hours later on horseback.

An even more dramatic demonstration happened in Great Britain in 1845. British railroad officials caught an escaping murderer by sending a message ahead to the next station, describing the criminal and giving his seat location. Without the telegraph the message would have had to follow along on the next train. By the time the information arrived, the murderer would have been long gone.

Within two years, telegraph wires

Hundreds of telegraph offices opened in a short time. Neatly arranged desks shown in New York City's Western Union office belie the bustle of activity that must have filled this room during work hours.

and stations dotted the American countryside. Presidents were sending telegraph messages, called telegrams, to communicate official announcements. Newspaper correspondents were using telegrams to flash the latest news back to their home offices in other states. Many newspapers even put the word "telegraph" into their names.

Underwater telegraph cables were laid between Britain and France in 1851. Ordinary citizens could go to the nearest telegraph station and pay operators to send messages to friends or relatives in distant towns. Unlike semaphore flags or telegraph towers, which were used only by armies, navies, and governments, the telegraph meant that instant communication for all people had truly arrived.

The electric telegraph was still not perfect. With Morse's device, two operators were needed to send and receive messages. Because messages had to be sent in written form, only the words themselves were transmitted. The telegraph could not convey tone of voice, sobs, or laughter. It could not allow the simultaneous give and take of live human conversation, nor give voice to spontaneous emotion.

Only thirty-two years after Morse sent his famous message, those problems would be solved. In 1876 another American amateur inventor, trying to improve Morse's electric telegraph, would astound the world with an even more amazing invention. He called it the telephone.

The Invention of the Telephone

In the years following Morse's invention, large telegraph companies formed in the United States and Europe. These companies trained operators in Morse code and built sending and receiving stations in every major city and town; thousands of miles of iron wire were strung on tall poles across many countries. Each wire could send only one message at a time, and that was not enough to handle the growing number of messages that more and more people and businesses wanted to send every day.

The telegraph companies needed to find ways to send a heavy volume of

American inventor Thomas Edison figured out a way to send four telegraph messages over a single wire.

messages cheaply and efficiently. Scientists and inventors tried to perfect methods of sending several messages over a single wire at the same time. Gradually, people like American inventor Thomas Edison invented ways to send two, then four, simultaneous messages through one telegraph wire. But four messages to a wire was still not enough to handle all the messages people wanted to send.

An Intriguing Idea

A young student at the University of Edinburgh in Scotland found himself intrigued by the experiments and improvements in the world of electric telegraphs. His name was Alexander Graham Bell. Bell planned to follow his grandfather and his father into a career of helping deaf people learn to speak. While studying to become a professor of speech science, Bell also consulted with scientific experts in Europe about what further advances could be made in telegraphy. Bell knew that the search was on for more powerful multiple-message-sending equipment. He wanted to invent a device that was even better than Edison's four-way telegraph message sender. He knew such an achievement would not only give him scientific fame but also make him rich.

In the 1860s young Bell read about a German experiment in which electricity, sent through a wire, vibrated musical

Part of Alexander Graham Bell's inspiration for the telephone came from his work with deaf students. Bell, top right, poses here with students and other staff for a class picture at the Boston School for the Deaf.

tuning forks on the far end of the wire. This happened because identical tuning forks were set up on the sending end of the wire. Their vibrations regulated the electrical impulses that traveled through the wire in just the right way to move the forks at the receiving end.

Bell realized that telegraph operators might be able to send dozens of simultaneous messages through a single wire by setting up a series of differently tuned tuning forks at both ends of a telegraph. On the sending end, several telegraph keys would make differently tuned forks vibrate at different speeds, or frequencies. It would be like tenor, alto, bass, and soprano voices all singing in harmony. The vibrations from all the forks would be sent as a jumble of electrical impulses through one telegraph wire.

At the receiving end, identical tuning forks attached to the telegraph wire would respond to only the impulses of their own frequency. Long or short notes, sent as separate vibrations to each fork, would then be turned into the dots and dashes of printed Morse code for written messages. In theory, a person could send as many messages at once as there are notes on a piano. Bell called this idea the harmonic telegraph.

The Harmonic Telegraph

Bell spent the next several years finishing his education, moving to America, and starting his career. He did not have time to work on his harmonic telegraph idea, but he never forgot about it. By 1870 twenty-four-year-old Professor Bell was teaching speech science at Boston University and tutoring deaf students. In his spare time he tried to perfect a harmonic telegraph.

It was during this time that an important improvement occurred to him. Instead of musical tuning forks, Bell substituted vibrating steel strips that resembled clarinet reeds. These steel reeds could be tuned more easily and precisely than tuning forks by adjusting the length of the part that vibrated. This improvement would help Bell set up precisely matched frequencies between the sending and receiving instruments.

Bell built a series of simple harmonic telegraphs, starting in 1874, using just three or four reeds at a time. His devices worked sometimes, but never very well or for very long. Electricity was still hard to understand and control. The mechanical adjustments were complicated and delicate. Bell continually tinkered with his designs and machinery, trying to perfect the mechanism.

At the same time, Bell began to have even grander ideas. He knew that the human voice makes its sound by us-

Bell was not content with his early harmonic telegraphs. So he set his sights on something better: a machine that could reproduce the sound of the human voice.

ing the muscles of the larynx to vibrate the air. What if Bell used electricity to make a steel reed vibrate exactly the same as a human larynx? Maybe a machine could reproduce the sound of a human voice! Then, by sending a controlling current of electricity through a wire to a distant reed, Bell's harmonic telegraph could send actual human speech miles away. Another reed on the receiving end would translate the electric current back into vibrations, which would reproduce the original sounds.

The prospect intrigued him, but Bell did not know how to make the electric power sent through the wire go up and down in just the right way to make the vibrating reed copy a human voice. Also, he did not know what kind of receiving device to put on the other end, to faithfully turn the changing electrical patterns back into the original sounds. While Bell continued to work on the harmonic telegraph, his thoughts kept returning to the new telephone, a device that would allow two people separated by some distance to talk to each other.

A New Competitor

In late 1874, Bell learned that a middle western electrician and inventor named Elisha Gray was also working on a harmonic telegraph. If Bell wanted to get the legal rights of ownership, the fame, and the money from this idea, he realized he would have to hurry. He needed a good working model so he could file for a patent, or the legal right to the use and profits from his invention.

Bell hired a gifted mechanic named Tom Watson to help him build better versions of his harmonic telegraph. Then he heard that Gray was also work-

SET SCREW

VIBRATING REED

ELECTRO MAGNET

HARMONIC TELEGRAPH TRANSMITTER

HARMONIC TELEGRAPH RECEIVER

Bell had financial backing to develop the harmonic telegraph pictured here. He began to lose interest in the device, however, as the idea for a telephone began to intrigue him.

ing on a telephone. This worried Bell. What he did not know was that Gray still had a way to go. Gray knew how to turn sounds into electrical current, but he could not think of a good way to turn the current back into sounds at the receiving end.

Nevertheless, Bell and Watson worked harder than ever on their har-

Tom Watson became Bell's working partner in the development of the telephone.

monic telegraph. They struggled with different kinds of batteries, wires, and electrical connections. Sometimes the different electrical frequencies of the tuning forks interfered with each other, resulting in no vibration, or only weak vibration, on the receiving end.

Finally, in early 1875, Bell had a model that was good enough to obtain a patent, even though it was not yet ready for commercial use. He traveled to Washington, D.C., to demonstrate a working multiple harmonic telegraph and apply for patents. The head of the Western Union Telegraph Company asked for a demonstration of Bell's device and seemed impressed. But he had also heard about Gray's work and wanted to see it before making any financial commitments.

Also during this trip, Bell met with Joseph Henry, whose crude electric telegraph had helped lead to Morse's working model. Bell told Henry about his telephone idea. "What do you advise me to do?" Bell asked. "Should I publish my telephone idea and let others work it out, or attempt to solve the problem myself?"

Henry, who was more than slightly

This replica of Bell and Watson's attic laboratory at 109 Court Street, Boston, is on display at New England Telephone Company's Boston offices.

jealous of all the money and fame Morse earned with the telegraph, said that Bell should definitely create a working telephone himself.

"But I lack the necessary electrical knowledge," Bell admitted.

"Then get it!" Henry urged him.

Thoughts Return to the Telephone

Back in Boston, Bell's friends—some of whom were helping to pay for his experiments—urged him to concentrate on the harmonic telegraph rather than the telephone. The harmonic telegraph seemed more likely to make a lot of money for these investors. Bell kept working on the harmonic telegraph, but his heart was not in it. His telephone idea and thoughts of Henry's encouragement kept distracting him.

For the first time, Bell began talking to his assistant about making a telephone. "Watson," said Bell, "if I can get a mechanism which will make a current

of electricity vary in its intensity [strength], as the air varies in density when a sound is passing through it, I can telegraph any sound—even the sound of speech."

Bell kept thinking about this problem. He realized that to make an electrical copy of a sound he would not have to change the amount of electricity going through the wire. Instead, he could leave the amount of electric current the same and change the amount of resistance in the wire.

Could resistance be changed with precision, in a way that caused electricity to copy the original sound? One answer came during a lucky accident on June 2, 1875, while Bell and Watson were struggling with their harmonic telegraph. Watson was in one room with one set of transmitting reeds, batteries, and magnets. A wire ran into the next room, where Bell had a matching set of receiving reeds, batteries, and magnets.

The harmonic telegraph was supposed to use electricity to make the reeds on the receiving end sound their own tones. On this day, though, in the process of tuning one of the reeds on the receiving end, Bell heard—very faintly—his reed broadcast the musical tone of a reed in Watson's room.

How had this happened? It seemed that one of Watson's reeds had become stuck. This caused a steady flow of electricity instead of the usual stop-and-start current ordinarily used to send dot-dash signals. Watson had plucked at the reed with his finger, trying to free it, but the reed stayed stuck, and it vibrated. The tiny waves of air pressure from Watson's plucked reed had, in turn, vibrated the constantly electrified wire. The movement of the wire inside the coil of an electromagnet changed the amount of resistance inside the wire, creating variable resistance.

Not only that, but the amount of variable resistance precisely matched the vibration of Watson's reed. The steady flow of electricity, changing in strength as the vibration changed, had traveled along the wire into Bell's room. There it had caused one of Bell's electromagnets to make its reed vibrate in precisely the same way, as if Bell's reed were being plucked by a ghost.

Steady Current and Vibrating Wires

Now Bell had a good idea of how to make a successful telephone. Steady current was part of the answer; a vibrating wire was another part of it. That very day, Bell and Watson began building a working model. In place of the collection of metal reeds, the telephone would have a vibrating diaphragm on each end of the wire. The diaphragm was a tightly stretched piece of skin or metal attached to the sending wire. Just

THIS MODEL OF BELL'S FIRST TELEPHONE IS A DUPLICATE OF THE INSTRUMENT THROUGH WHICH SPEECH SOUNDS WERE FIRST TRANSMITTED ELECTRICALLY, 1875.

A replica of Bell's telephone, the first instrument to transmit speech sounds electrically.

like a human larynx, the diaphragm vibrated easily at any frequency in response to varying air pressure.

On the sending end, the speaker's voice would make the diaphragm vibrate. This in turn would make the wire vibrate. The electric current would carry those changing vibrations along the wire, where they would make the second diaphragm vibrate on the receiving end. These tiny vibrations would move the air near the listener's ear, reproducing the original sound.

Although Bell's theory was correct, putting it into practice was difficult because he and Watson were still beginners when it came to electricity. Over the next several months, the two inventors tried various types of batteries, electromagnetic coils, and materials for diaphragms.

In January 1876 Bell realized there was a better way to create variable resistance. He did not have to rely on only the original sound to vibrate the wire. Instead, he could send the electrical impulses through liquid, in addition to a wire, as the current traveled from sender to receiver.

Although the combination of electricity and water is often dangerous, Bell knew that liquid has one very useful property. It conducts electricity, and the amount of resistance changes according to how much contact the ends of the wire have with the water. If a vibrating wire were dipped into a bowl of water, Bell reasoned, the current could go from the wire, through the water, then back into another wire whose end was in the same water. The water would cause the amount of resistance to vary precisely according to the amount of vibration by the wire.

Telegraphing Human Speech

Bell and Watson began building a telephone whose wire ends were dipped into a bowl of water. Bell also described his idea to the U.S. Patent Office and asked for a patent. Bell knew that working telephones in offices and houses could not depend on this clumsy arrangement. His first goal was to discover and patent the scientific principles that allowed him to telegraph human speech. He could work out the practical details later.

Through January and February of 1876, Watson built several new models that almost worked. At times, Bell wrote later, they would hear "confused muttering" or mumbling, voicelike sounds. After a month, Bell could sing a tune on one end and Watson could recognize

Sketches from Bell's notebook show his ideas for controlling electrical resistance. This included dipping a vibrating wire into a bowl of water.

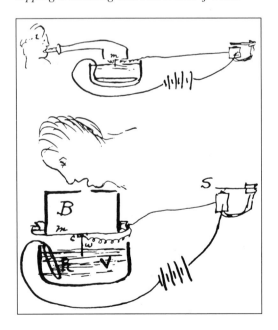

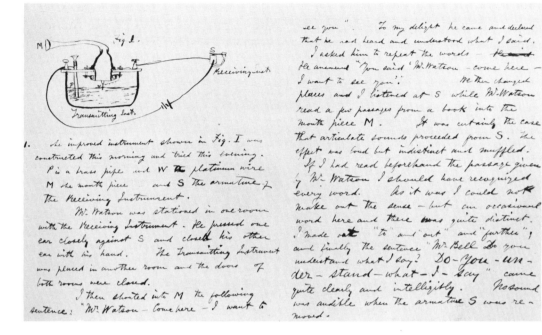

Bell's historic first telephone conversation—recorded for all time in this page from his notebook—delighted the inventor and his assistant. They had finally invented the telephone.

the melody on the other. They still could not transmit a spoken voice clearly. They kept trying new combinations of materials.

The Patent Office granted Bell's patent on March 7, 1876—before anyone actually demonstrated that his idea would work. Not until March 10, 1876, did Bell and Watson come up with the exact combination of delicate materials to transmit a human voice by electricity.

The first telephone looked like a small, upright megaphone, with the bottom end mounted into three brass rings and supported by brass tripod legs. The wide, open end of the tube pointed upward. Inside the brass rings was a very thin iron disk, used as the diaphragm. The tripod's legs were set into a square wooden base. The speaker leaned over the tube and shouted into it. On the receiving end, the listener held his ear over the same kind of iron disk and tube, which now served as the listening device.

First Words

Bell sat in the attic of Watson's machine shop with the transmitter. Watson was on the ground floor with the receiver. When the batteries were hooked up, Bell dipped the end of the transmitting wire very slightly into the bowl of water. He then shouted into the speaking tube: "Mr. Watson! Come here! I want you!"

Downstairs, Watson heard these exact words come out of his hearing tube. He rushed upstairs, burst into Bell's room, and exclaimed, "Mr. Bell, I understood what you said!" Bell asked Watson to repeat the sentence exactly, and Watson did so. Their telephone worked!

Bell's new telephone won first prize as the best new invention at the 1876 Philadelphia Centennial Exposition. A replica of that telephone—its transmitter (at left) and its receiver (at right)—is shown here. A painting (below) depicts the exciting moment when Watson rushed into Bell's room to report that he had heard Bell speak over the telephone.

Bell immediately ran downstairs to listen, while Watson remained upstairs to read from a book into the speaking tube. "It certainly was the case that articulate sounds proceeded from [the vibrating diaphragm]," Bell later wrote. "The effect was loud but indistinct and muffled. If I had read beforehand the passage given by Mr. Watson, I should have recognized every word. As it was, I

Actors portray Bell and Watson discussing the invention that would usher in a new era of communication.

could not make out the sense [of the written passage], but an occasional word here and there was quite distinct. I made out 'to' and 'out' and 'further'; and finally the sentence 'Mr. Bell do you understand what I say?'" Then Watson repeated slowly, and with great emphasis, "Do you un-der-stand-what-I-say?"

They tinkered and tested some more, adjusting the pressure of the wire on the diaphragm, trying new contacts of wire and liquid. Watson heard Bell ask "How do you do?" and he heard Bell sing "God Save the Queen."

Bell was delighted. "This is a great day with me," he wrote that night in a letter to his father. "I feel I have at last struck the solution to a great problem—and the day is coming when telegraph wires will be laid on to houses just like water or gas—and friends converse with each other without leaving home."

Bell was right. In two short years, telephones would equip tens of thousands of houses and offices across America. Not everyone could see the use for this new invention at first. Bell and his friends had a struggle ahead of them.

The Toy Becomes a Tool

The early telephone looked like a wooden box with a cone attached to it. Talking required shouting into the cone. Listening required moving quickly to position an ear next to the same cone. Sometimes it was hard to understand what was being said when using that early, primitive telephone. The sound was full of static, like an AM radio broadcast during a thunderstorm. This static resulted from interference in electrical patterns. Interference was caused by jiggling wires, other telegraph lines, or other electrical instruments nearby. Even under the best conditions, sending electric current through a bowl of water just did not work very well.

Bell and Watson kept tinkering with the telephone. They replaced the bowl of water with a small electric generator. The generator, which used permanent magnets, was called a magneto. They attached a vibrating steel reed to the diaphragm. This version was more reliable than the one that used water, but the sound on the receiving end was weak.

The two inventors felt hopeful about their telephone one day, despairing the next. "During the summer of 1876," Watson later recalled, "the telephone was talking so well that one did not have to ask the other man to say it over again more than three or four times before one could understand it quite well, if the sentences were simple." By November Watson said the telephone "would work moderately well over a short line, but the apparatus was delicate and complicated, and it did not talk distinctly enough for practical use."

Marvel or Joke?

America's one-hundredth birthday was in 1876. To celebrate, the nation held a Centennial Exhibition in Philadelphia that summer. Bell took his telephone to the exhibition and won first prize for

Bell's exhibitor's pass for the Centennial Exhibition. His telephone won first place.

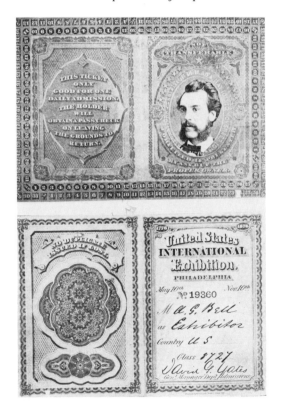

The Centennial Exhibition attracted visitors from near and far. This sketch depicts the hall where Bell displayed his telephone (shown in inset at right).

the best new invention. The judges included Bell's friend, Joseph Henry, and a British physicist named Lord Kelvin, the most distinguished scientist of the time. They said they were "delighted and astonished" to hear and recognize words and sentences, and even the distinctive character of their individual voices, over the telephone. Lord Kelvin called Bell's invention "the greatest marvel hitherto achieved by the electric telegraph" and said that with more power and a better design, people separated by hundreds of miles would one day talk to each other.

Not everyone was so excited about the telephone's potential. On October 5, 1876, a story in the *New York Tribune* asked, "Of what use is such an invention? Well, there may be occasions of state [government situations] when it is necessary for officials who are far apart to talk with each other, without the interferences of [a telegraph] operator. Or some lover may wish to pop the question [propose marriage] directly into the ear of a lady and hear for himself her reply, though miles away; it is not hard for us to guess how courtships will be conducted in the twentieth century. . . . Music can be readily transmitted. Think of serenading by telegraph!"

To that *Tribune* reporter, the telephone was a joke. The businessmen who ran the Western Union Telegraph Company did not see much future in telephones, either. Bell tried to interest Western Union in his invention, but company officials did not even want to see a demonstration. They said, "We cannot use an electrical toy."

Drawing In the Public

Bell thought that maybe he should form his own company and make telephones himself. Meanwhile, in the early months of 1877, he started giving public demonstrations of the telephone in Boston and nearby cities. Bell drew audiences of five hundred people who came to see him stand on a stage and talk by telephone to Watson, who was on the other end of a telegraph wire twenty miles away with a second unit.

"Hoy, ahoy, Mr. Watson!" Bell would shout into the phone, like a sailor hailing a distant ship. "Will you speak to this audience in Salem?" Watson's voice would come back through the cone: "How do you do, ladies and gentlemen? What do you think of the telephone?" Then Watson would tell his distant audience about the temperature and weather at his location and sing songs like "Auld Lang Syne" and "Yankee Doodle Dandy."

Audiences were amazed. "It is indeed difficult, hearing the sounds out of the mysterious box, to wholly resist the notion that the powers of darkness are somehow in league with it," wrote the *Providence Press*. The *Boston Advertiser* praised the telephone's "weirdness and novelty"; the *Boston Herald* found the telephone "almost supernatural."

Bolstered by these demonstrations, public interest in the telephone increased. By the summer of 1877, Bell had at last found the financial backing

Bell and Watson amazed audiences with their telephone demonstrations. A sketch depicts one such demonstration, with Watson in Boston and Bell twenty miles away in Salem.

The first telephone Bell sold commercially was a wooden-box model. It was eventually replaced with a hand-held model.

to start his own business. Bell, Watson, and two other investors became partners in the Bell Telephone Company on July 11. They hired professional managers to run the company, with Bell and Watson on the board of directors.

That summer the first commercial telephones were sold to a bank. The bank's officers paid a $40 a year rental and maintenance of a set of phones. There were no private telegraph wires going to people's houses, so the bankers had to pay at least $150 a mile to have private lines of iron wire put up on poles between their homes and the office.

The early telephone was a big improvement on the telegraph. It allowed actual transmission of human speech, resulting in two-way conversation. The telegraph had permitted only one-way transmission of written messages. Still, the early telephone was impractical, compared to today's equipment. Two people could talk to each other only if their telephones were directly connected with a special wire. Also, telephones did not ring automatically like

they do today. The caller had to tap the unit with a small hammer, setting off vibrations that caused the receiving telephone to make a buzzing sound. This sound signaled an incoming call.

Catching the Public Eye

Despite these drawbacks, people began ordering telephones. By the fall of 1877, more than six hundred houses and offices had telephones, all using private lines. The first telephone directory was published in New Haven, Connecticut, in 1878; it contained fifty listings, including three doctors and two dentists. The fact that the doctors were listed prompted more people to order telephones. Many users said they felt much safer knowing they could call a doctor in case of emergency.

This did not always work smoothly, however. Several doctors and a drug store were connected to the same line in Hartford, Connecticut. If one of the users tapped the telephone to signal a call, all of the telephones on the line

Author and humorist Mark Twain was one of the first celebrities to have a telephone installed in his home.

comedy writers named Gilbert and Sullivan included the telephone in their new operetta, *H.M.S. Pinafore*, a story about the British navy. Even magazine cartoonists used the new invention as a subject.

Thanks to all this activity and publicity, Bell Telephone's business finally took off. During the next year the company installed more than ten thousand phones. Most of them were in New England. Many were in private homes, but many businesses also ordered phones. Telephones began turning up in the most unlikely places—inside mine shafts, attached to underwater cables,

The first telephone exchange opened in January 1878 in New Haven, Connecticut. It published this directory the following month.

would buzz in all of the houses and offices, and everyone would answer at the same time.

Famous people also began ordering telephones. Congressman James Garfield, who later became president of the United States, had one installed in his home. Writer Mark Twain got one for his big house in Hartford, although he joked about its usefulness. "Here we have been hollering 'shut up' to our neighbors for centuries," Twain teased the installers, "and now you fellows come along and seek to complicate matters. If Bell had invented a muffler or gag, he would have done a real service."

When Bell and his wife Mabel traveled to England for their honeymoon, Queen Victoria asked the inventor to demonstrate his machine. The queen liked it so much that she asked for her own telephone set. Two British musical

LIST OF SUBSCRIBERS.

New Haven District Telephone Company.

OFFICE 219 CHAPEL STREET.

February 21, 1878.

Residences.	*Stores, Factories, &c.*
Rev. JOHN E. TODD.	O. A. DORMAN.
J. B. CARRINGTON.	STONE & CHIDSEY.
H. B. BIGELOW.	NEW HAVEN FLOUR CO. State St.
C. W. SCRANTON.	" " " Cong. ave.
GEORGE W. COY.	" " " Grand St.
G. L. FERRIS.	" " " Fair Haven.
H. P. FROST.	ENGLISH & MERSICK.
M. F. TYLER.	New Haven FOLDING CHAIR CO.
I. H. BROMLEY.	H. HOOKER & CO.
GEO. E. THOMPSON.	W. A. ENSIGN & SON.
WALTER LEWIS.	H. B. BIGELOW & CO.
	C. COWLES & CO.
Physicians.	C. S. MERSICK & CO.
Dr. E. L. R. THOMPSON.	SPENCER & MATTHEWS.
Dr. A. E. WINCHELL.	PAUL ROESSLER.
Dr. C. S. THOMSON, Fair Haven.	E. S. WHEELER & CO.
	ROLLING MILL CO.
Dentists.	APOTHECARIES HALL.
Dr. E. S. GAYLORD.	E. A. GESSNER.
Dr. R. F. BURWELL.	AMERICAN TEA CO.
Miscellaneous.	*Meat & Fish Markets.*
REGISTER PUBLISHING CO	W. H. HITCHINGS, City Market.
POLICE OFFICE.	GEO. E. LUM, " "
POST OFFICE.	A. FOOTE & CO.
MERCANTILE CLUB.	STRONG, HART & CO.
QUINNIPIAC CLUB.	
F. V. McDONALD, Yale News.	*Hack and Boarding Stable.*
SMEDLEY BROS & CO.	CRITTENDEN & CARTER.
M. F. TYLER, Law Chambers	BARKER & RANSOM.

Office open from 6 A M to 2 A M.
After March 1st, this Office will be open all night.

HOW A TELEPHONE CARRIES SOUND

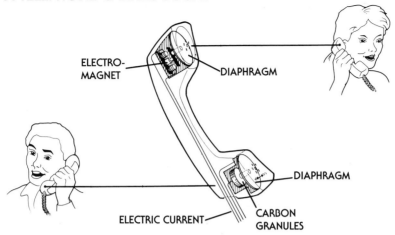

ELECTRO-MAGNET

DIAPHRAGM

DIAPHRAGM

ELECTRIC CURRENT

CARBON GRANULES

In a basic telephone, the part that most people refer to as the "receiver" is actually a receiver and transmitter. The mouthpiece transmits sound and the earpiece receives it.

The transmitter contains a thin metal disk called a diaphragm. When sound waves strike the diaphragm, it vibrates against a chamber filled with tiny grains of carbon. The vibrations vary according to the sound. Strong sounds send more electric current through the carbon chamber; weak sounds send less. Whether strong or weak, the electric current copies the pattern of the sound waves and then travels through the carbon chamber and over a wire to another telephone.

Like the transmitter, the earpiece receiver also contains a diaphragm. Attached to this diaphragm is a permanent magnet and an electromagnet. When electric current reaches the receiver, it activates the electromagnet. The force of the electromagnet pulls on the diaphragm, opposing the steady pull of the permanent magnet. The changes in magnetic pull cause the diaphragm to vibrate. These vibrations re-create the sound waves made by the caller's voice. The sound waves strike the listener's ear and the listener hears the caller's words.

and on railroads. Watson himself donned a deep-sea diving suit to help install a telephone at the bottom of Boston Harbor, to be used by builders and repairmen on the bottom of the sea floor!

At last even Western Union realized that telephones were going to be big business. The company already owned thousands of miles of wire that stretched across the country. It had millions of dollars to invest. Western Union's owners reasoned that adding telephones to their existing telegraph system was a logical extension of their existing business, and it would be very profitable. The company decided to enter into competition with Bell Telephone.

Needing equipment, Western Union bought the rights to Elisha Gray's telephone patents. (Gray had filed legal papers describing his untested idea for a similar invention soon after Bell obtained his first patent.) Next the company hired another young inventor, Thomas Edison, who came up with a much better transmitter than Bell and Watson had thought of.

Instead of messy bowls of water or weak magnetos and steel reeds, Edison used a carbon "button" for the telephone's diaphragm. Inside this button were small grains of carbon. As the weak and strong sound waves from a human voice hit the diaphragm, the changing pressure caused the carbon grains to pack tightly together or spread loosely apart. The changing density of the carbon grains provided a tidy way to create variable resistance. The changing resistance affected the electricity that flowed from the battery, through the diaphragm, into the sending wire. At the receiving end, another carbon button worked the same way, causing the electric current to vibrate the diaphragm and copy the original sound.

Carbon buttons vastly improved the telephone's sound quality. Users did not have to shout into the telephone anymore for someone at the other end to hear every word. The mechanism was simpler and more reliable. Improved versions of Edison's carbon button are still used in telephones today.

Now Western Union was ready to challenge Bell Telephone. The fight began. Western Union started making and selling its own telephones with Edison transmitters, while telling people that Bell telephones did not work well. Western Union tried to push Bell out of business by spreading the word that Bell had a questionable legal claim to the telephone. In fact, Bell had a stronger claim than did Western Union, which should have been paying Bell for permission to make, sell, and operate any telephones at all.

Bell Telephone fought back by improving its telephones. The company purchased rights to better transmitters based on Edison's work but created by other inventors. These improved trans-

The ease of using a telephone grew when inventors found a way to separate the mouthpiece from the earpiece. This allowed the user to speak and listen without having to switch the instrument back and forth between the mouth and ear. Many different designs were sold, including the two shown here.

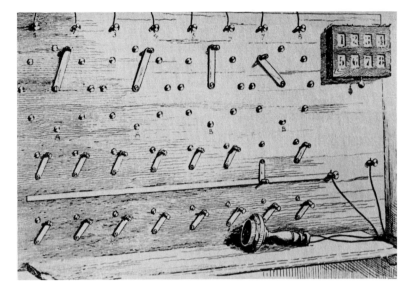

The invention of the switchboard enabled operators to connect two telephone lines into one temporary circuit. This ended the need for separate lines for every telephone and the necessity of sharing lines with other telephone users.

mitters performed even better because they made it possible to have a receiver, or earpiece, separated from the transmitter, or mouthpiece. The telephone became more convenient to use. Also, Watson eliminated the small hammer for signaling an incoming call. Instead, he added a crank on the side of the telephone. Callers picked up the receiver and turned the crankshaft; this made the telephone on the other end buzz.

Having a telephone that worked well and was easy to use was an important step in better communication. For telephones to be really useful, though, a vast network of support services had to be created. These included better wires, telephone offices, telephone operators, and devices to switch calls from one line to another.

The first important support service for telephones came about when a man named George Coy invented the central exchange. This was a central office that worked as a transfer station for electrical impulses going to and from different telephones. All the telephone lines in a city or town went to this exchange.

When a call came in, a telephone operator worked like a railroad switchman—except that instead of helping trains switch tracks, the operator switched the incoming call to the desired telephone line. The operator then sent an electric current to activate the buzzer of the destination telephone to let the party know a call was coming in.

The operation was accomplished at a switchboard with a simple but flexible system of plugs and jacks. These tools allowed operators to connect the lines of any two telephones into a single, temporary circuit. No longer were dozens or hundreds of individual lines needed to connect telephones directly to each other. No longer did everybody have to share the same line and receive the same call at the same time.

Connecting with Central

The first central exchange began service in New Haven, Connecticut on January 28, 1878, less than two years after the first telephone conversation. This exchange connected twenty-one Bell Telephone users. The second central exchange opened three days later in Meriden, Connecticut.

Suddenly everybody wanted a telephone. Doctors, dentists, police departments, fire departments, store owners, and home owners all realized that telephones could be easy and fun to use, convenient for business, and fashionable for social purposes. By June 1878 the number of Bell telephones in service had grown to 10,755.

The competition between Bell and Western Union became fierce in February 1878. That month Western Union opened its first central exchange office in San Francisco, California—just days after the very first Bell exchange had begun operating. Western Union was able to operate so quickly by using its existing telegraph wires and operators at its local telegraph station. Western Union opened a dozen more telephone exchanges that year in various telegraph offices across the country. Bell Telephone opened exchanges in each city as quickly as possible after Western Union did. With all its money, Western Union was determined to steamroll

A drawing depicts a Western Union telephone exchange in the late 1800s. Western Union used its network of operators and telephone cables to compete fiercely with Bell Telephone.

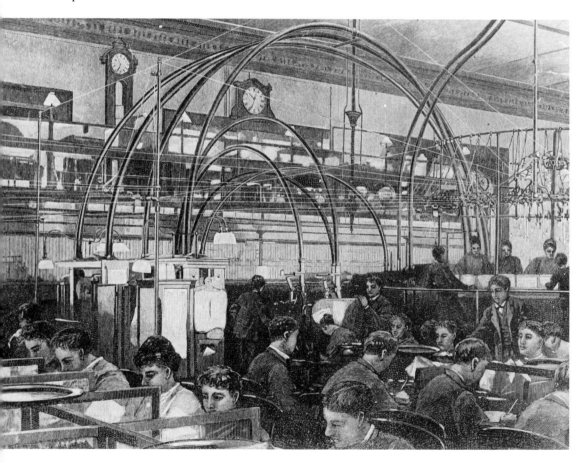

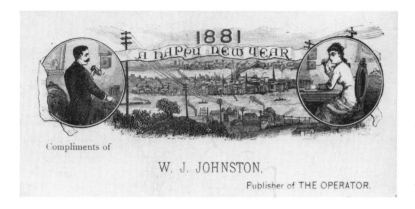

1881
A HAPPY NEW YEAR

Compliments of

W. J. JOHNSTON,

Publisher of THE OPERATOR.

Businesses were quick to capitalize on the popularity of telephones. Advertisements and even greeting cards like the one shown here often featured people using telephones.

right over the smaller Bell Telephone. In May the competition took an ugly turn when Western Union sued Bell Telephone for patent infringement. Western Union claimed that Bell Telephone was making money on an invention owned by Western Union.

Moving On

Bell tried not to let the lawsuit bother him. "The more fame a man gets for an invention, the more he becomes a target for the world to shoot at," he said. Bell and his lawyers produced many documents, including his first patents, his personal diaries, and even his private love letters to Mabel Hubbard before their marriage to prove that Alexander Graham Bell was the true inventor of the telephone.

Supported by overwhelming evidence, Bell won the case decisively. In November 1879, Western Union agreed to give up its telephone business, its patents, and even its big telephone manufacturing plant to the Bell Telephone Company.

By then Bell and Watson had grown tired of being businessmen. They still loved the excitement of learning and discovery, but running a company bored them. Just three years after Bell Telephone was founded, both men resigned from the board of directors. Bell spent the rest of his life working on speech science and creating many other inventions. Watson became an adventurer and world traveler.

Although they left it to others to continue improving and extending the telephone system, Bell and Watson had finished their work. They created the first working telephone, then made sure it was accepted as a vitally important tool. By the time they retired from the telephone industry, their invention was the world's fastest-growing and most-important method of communication.

Telephones Reach Across America

Bell Telephone's victory over Western Union gave the company fourteen more years to do business as a monopoly. That meant Bell could operate without competition before its patents expired in 1893. The firm spent those years making better telephones, improving transmission quality, and linking cities with long-distance lines and equipment. When the telephone industry became open to free competition, Bell wanted to be as strong as possible so it could defeat any rivals.

Bell Develops Better Telephones

The telephones themselves were the first area for improvement. Bell did away with the leaky, built-in battery, the signal buzzer, and the primitive wooden box with a single speaking and listening tube that sat on a desk top. Instead, Bell Telephone developed a handsome, wall-mounted box of varnished wood, with ringing bells that signaled an incoming call. The speaking tube was permanently fixed to the front of the wooden body of the phone. A hand-held earpiece receiver rested on a switch hook on the side of the cabinet.

When not in use, the hook stayed down, and the line was closed. When the customer picked up the earpiece receiver, the hook popped up and opened the line to the central exchange. Meanwhile, the battery power

to run the telephone came over the electric wire from the central exchange, which people referred to as "Central."

Service was the next area for improvement. Central exchanges were initially staffed by teenage boys. Many had worked as telegraph operators, so the transition seemed natural. But this arrangement did not last long. Young men in those days were expected to be a bit rough in manners and speech. This was fine for unseen, unheard telegraph operators.

Such behavior was a disaster in a busy telephone exchange, with dozens of fellows crashing into each other,

Switchboard operators make connections in a nineteenth-century telephone exchange office.

Women began replacing young boys as telephone operators in the 1870s. By 1911, when this photograph was taken, most of these jobs were held by women.

shouting and cursing—sometimes at the callers. Bell Telephone decided that women, thought to be patient and well-mannered, would make much better operators. The company hired Emma Nut, a former telegraph operator, as the first female telephone operator in September 1878. More women followed and telephone customers said service was much better. Today women and men work as telephone operators.

Better Wire and Clearer Connections

Even with better equipment and polite operators, placing telephone calls still presented problems in the 1870s and 1880s. The static and interference were terrible. Poor sound quality arose from many sources. Iron wire had been fine

for electric telegraph communication, but it was a noisy and unreliable carrier of telephone impulses. Bell began replacing the iron with copper wire, which was a better conductor of electricity.

A new problem cropped up as electric power stations and electric lighting began appearing in American cities. All of this power caused terrific electrical interference in telephone wires. Still more interference came from electric trolley cars, electric street lamps, and thunderstorms. As a result, static hissed and roared on the telephone lines, drowning out people's conversations. "Such a jangle of meaningless noises had never been heard by human ears!" wrote one phone user of the day. "There were spluttering and bubbling, jerking

With telephones spreading to cities across the United States, the market for wire and other essential parts grew.

THE WIRE
=== OF ===
QUALITY

TELEPHONE WIRE

BEST BY EVERY TEST

Dubbed by leading users Plain talk and long distance wire because of its superior quality

WRITE FOR FREE SAMPLE AND MAKE COMPARISON—BE CONVINCED

Handled by Leading Supply Houses or Sold Direct.

Indiana Steel & Wire Co.
MUNCIE - INDIANA

A photograph of a New York City street in 1887 shows the forest of telephone poles and wires that had sprung up only ten years after Bell introduced his invention.

and rasping, whistling and screaming."

The solution came in 1881 when a Bell engineer named John Carty found a way to insulate telephone lines. Until this time the telephone used a one-wire circuit that diverted unused power into the ground, where random interference from other sources could enter the telephone wires. Carty created a two-wire circuit that sent unused power back to the original source over the second wire. This system did not have any open connections that other electrical sources could enter. Except during the very worst thunderstorms, static nearly disappeared from local calls. "I will never forget the remarkable change which it made," said John Carty.

Carty's solution was expensive because it used twice as much wire as a single-wire circuit. Also, the more wire that was strung up on poles, the uglier cities became. Greater amounts of wire

also made telephone lines vulnerable to ice formation in winter time, and when enough ice formed on the wires, they came crashing down. Not only was this dangerous to passersby on the street below, but it knocked out telephone service for days on end. To solve these problems, the telephone company eventually began burying its wires in cities, although wires remained strung high up on poles in the countryside.

More Telephones in More Cities

While working to improve transmission quality inside each city, Bell also labored to bring service to as many cities and towns as possible. After winning its patent suit, Bell bought all of Western Union's working telephones and acquired its customers across the country.

Telephones underwent many changes to make them easier to use. The model shown here appeared in 1886.

tination telephones in 1892. A new device allowed callers to dial numbers themselves, rather than asking operators to connect them to other lines. This device was called an automatic dialer. Early versions used two pushbuttons that the caller had to push many, many times to send the right number to the exchange office. Later versions used an easier rotary dial mechanism, which remained the standard for many decades.

With better telephones, copper wires, underground cables, operators, and automatic dialers, telephone service had improved greatly. But it remained strictly local: Callers could reach telephones in their own cities, but to communicate with other cities, they still had to send mail or telegrams.

Extending the Telephone's Reach

After every major city had local telephone service, the next logical step was to let callers reach telephones in other cities. Long-distance service began in 1892 from Chicago to New York. In 1893 Boston-Chicago service began.

In 1885 American Bell formed a new subsidiary called American Telephone & Telegraph (AT&T) for the special purpose of building a nationwide network of long distance lines. The company believed that having such a network would keep it first in the telephone business when Bell's patents expired. American Bell would remain the owner and operator of the local telephone networks in each town and city.

At first, city-to-city service suffered the same problems that had once plagued local calling: poor sound quality, electrical interference, and the old

Bell combined the two systems in 1880 and formed American Bell Telephone Company, with a total of 61,000 telephones in the United States. By 1881 the number of telephones more than doubled, to 132,692. Almost every American city with a population of ten thousand or more had its own telephone exchange.

With more telephones in use and more calls being made every day, the work load on operators also increased. To make it easier for operators to connect calls to the right destination telephones, Bell began assigning numbers to each telephone. This made it possible for machines to begin doing some of the work of connecting callers to des-

Bell places the first long-distance call over the newly opened line from New York to Chicago in 1892.

Bell Telephone president Theodore Vail resigned in 1887 over a dispute with profit-hungry members of Bell's board of directors.

problem of resistance. Static increased and sound faded out as the electrical impulses traveled over distances of hundreds of miles. Engineers at AT&T began work on possible solutions to these problems.

Problems for Bell

Before Bell's engineers solved the technical problems of long-distance calling, the company ran into two serious problems. First, Bell's board of directors got greedy. Since the Bell patents allowed them to run the telephone industry without competition for many years, the directors were free to charge excessively

By 1900, every small town in America had telephone service, and one in sixteen Americans had a telephone.

firms did exactly that, and many independent manufacturers built equipment for them.

The Era of Competition

Competition brought many benefits to telephone users. Rates were lowered to attract customers. Bell and independent companies extended telephone service to every small town and village in the United States. By 1900 some 800,000 American telephones belonged to the Bell system, and another 600,000 were owned by the independent companies. That amounted to one telephone for every sixteen American citizens, far more telephones for the population than any other country had.

Another benefit of competition was that engineers created another round of technical improvements in the telephone, its components, and support technology. Bell changed from big,

high prices to customers. They kept most of the profits to enrich stockholders instead of using them to improve the system. Customers resented this policy.

Some state legislatures tried to force prices down, but the Bell directors treated government like an enemy, refusing to comply or even to provide information. Bell president Theodore Vail resigned over these issues in 1887. Vail was a practical idealist who believed that short-term profiteering and antigovernment attitude would hurt the quality of service and would also hurt Bell's long-term success.

Then Bell ran into a second problem: Its patents expired in 1893. The telephone industry became a wide-open marketplace. Any company could now put up wires, hire operators, set up exchanges, print directories, and offer telephone service. During the next few years, some six thousand independent

In the early 1900s, the Chesapeake & Potomac Telephone Company offered its subscribers rotary-dial telephones like this one. The dial, detailed at right, was inscribed with directions for use.

boxy, wall-mounted wooden telephones to smaller, metal, desktop units. Automatic dialers went onto more and more telephones.

These changes made telephones easier and cheaper for customers to use. Yet competition also brought many problems. The independent companies were small and lacked financing, so they offered only local telephone service. This meant that subscribers to non-Bell systems could not make long-distance calls.

Competition also created chaos. Some towns had as many as three different telephone systems, with three directories, three sets of wires that were not interconnected, and three different central exchange offices.

Callers could not talk to everyone in town unless they had two or three separate telephones in their houses, connected to two or three separate services. They would also have to pay two or three annual fees, which wiped out the savings gained from competition.

Bell slowly won this battle against the independent telephone companies because people gradually realized that Bell was the only service with a long-distance network. Eventually the independents had to sell out to Bell, or pay a fee to connect to Bell's AT&T long-distance network.

Coast-to-Coast Telephone Calling

The quality of long-distance transmissions began to improve when AT&T invented and installed loading coils. These coils were a new kind of battery, stationed every mile or so along the telephone wires. The loading coil helped re-

On June 17, 1914, workers on the Nevada-Utah border mount the final pole needed to complete the first transcontinental telephone line.

duce static. The coil also helped keep the electricity from dying out as it went farther and farther along the wire. Thanks to loading coils, customers could have long-distance conversations from New York to Denver, and all points between, starting in 1904. The sound was still faint, though.

In 1907 AT&T rehired Theodore Vail, the telephone company president who had quit twenty years earlier. Vail went right back to demanding equipment improvements and better service. He also insisted on making all of the company's business public and on cooperating with government regulators. In addition, Vail insisted that AT&T in-

TRIODE VACUUM TUBE

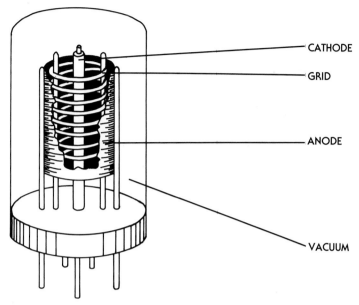

CATHODE

GRID

ANODE

VACUUM

The triode vacuum tube, invented in 1906, opened the way for long-distance telephoning. It provided the means for amplifying or boosting weak telephone signals. Telephone signals weaken as they move along telephone lines. When this occurs, sound quality worsens.

The triode vacuum tube, or repeater as it is known in the telephone industry, strengthens telephone signals by regulating the electric current which carries the signals. This work occurs inside a vacuum, or airless chamber. As electric current flows through the tube, the cathode emits or gives off electrons and the anode collects the electrons. The grid controls the amount of electrons flowing to the anode. By controlling the flow of electrons, the vacuum tube regulates the strength of electric current flowing between telephones.

vest money in the technology that made possible the first coast-to-coast telephone conversation.

That historic conversation occurred on January 25, 1915. A young inventor named Dr. Lee De Forest had invented the vacuum tube: a sealed, airless, glass bulb containing electrical wires. This tube was able to send and strengthen electrical current and to control it precisely. It meant that electrical impulses could be made strong enough to send a phone call three thousand miles, or the distance from one coast of the United States to the other.

By setting up a series of vacuum tube repeaters across the country, AT&T connected President Woodrow Wilson in the White House to a telephone in San Francisco. Wilson first greeted the governor of California. Then in New York City, sixty-nine-year-old Alexander Graham Bell used an original 1876 telephone, connected to the same circuit. President Wilson listened in as Bell spoke.

"They have asked me to repeat the

Bell poses with Bell System and New York City officials at the placing of the first transcontinental call on January 25, 1915. The link between New York and San Francisco was acclaimed as a great technical achievement.

first words I spoke over the telephone thirty-nine years ago," Bell said. "Mr. Watson, come here, I want you!"

In San Francisco, Tom Watson was also on the same circuit as the president and the governor of California. He cheerfully answered back: "I'd be happy to come, Mr. Bell—but it would take me a week to get there now!"

Watson's good-natured reply showed how far the telephone had come in just four decades. People separated by three thousand miles, or by a week of railroad travel, could talk instantly, plainly, and easily. After that day in 1915, telephones truly blanketed all of America.

■ ■ ■ ■ ■ ■ ■ ■ ■ ■ CHAPTER **5**

Building a Global Network

With a national telephone network in place, it was time to start extending the telephone's reach beyond the borders of the United States. The telegraph had already been sending Morse code messages back and forth across the Atlantic Ocean for fifty years, helping Americans conduct business and diplomacy with other nations. In the years 1914 to 1918, with so many countries fighting in World War I, the telephone needed to catch up to the telegraph.

The next big steps were to build national telephone networks in other countries, to extend the American network across the oceans to those countries, and finally to link all the telephone networks in the world by radio technology. However, these steps did not happen in a simple, orderly sequence. Progress occurred in many areas simultaneously and without coordination since so many people and countries were involved and since there was no central director with a dominant goal. Each industry, each branch of science, and each country pursued its own goals, at its own pace, in its own way.

Speaking Across an Ocean

A transatlantic telephone call came first. This transmission did not use wires, which were the medium for long-distance calls in America and for telegraph messages between nations. Instead, the first transatlantic call was sent over radio waves, and this medium was to become the standard technology for international calls from the 1930s to the 1950s.

Pushed by Theodore Vail, AT&T engineers used radio waves in October 1915 to broadcast a short test message from a telephone in Norfolk, Virginia, to another telephone in Paris, France. The event was not at all dramatic, with technicians on each end of the line who said nothing memorable. The Eiffel Tower in Paris was used as a giant radio antenna to collect the radio waves, which were then translated back into

The Eiffel Tower in Paris was used as a radio antenna to receive the first transatlantic telephone call, which was sent by radio waves.

the proper electrical patterns for telephone sounds.

Despite the lack of human drama, this call was viewed as an important technical accomplishment. Radios and radio technology were still fairly new. Home radio sets and radio stations did not even exist yet. Because of this lack of supporting technology, international telephoning did not become practical for everyday use for another dozen years. Nevertheless, AT&T's 1915 experiment showed what direction the telephone would eventually take to achieve worldwide scope.

The Bell Battalions

When America entered World War I in 1917, the Bell company formed volunteer battalions to help the U.S. Army Signal Corps, the part of the army that specialized in communications. As American troops sailed to France, American industry also went to war, supplying planes, tanks, guns, and cannons—and 273 central exchanges built in France by the 7,500 men and women of the "Bell battalions." American troops used these exchanges to telephone orders and intelligence between frontline troops and to communicate with headquarters.

France already had some telephones of its own, but its network was not so vast, nor built so quickly, as that of the U.S. Army. The army's demonstration of efficiency helped all European countries develop their own telephone networks after the war ended.

The 1920s were years of growth and prosperity for almost every industrial country in the world. It was during this time that European countries began to catch up with the United States in terms of the number of telephones and quality of service.

Some countries had quite a way to

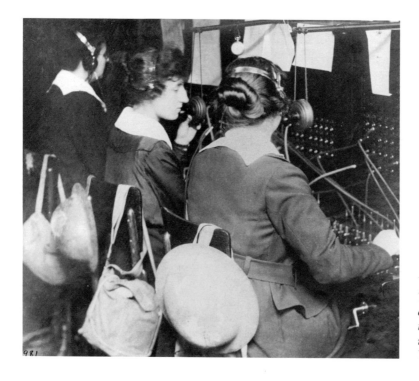

Volunteers from Bell Telephone help the war effort by operating telephone switchboards in France during World War I.

French onlookers gather to watch American telephone workers hook up telephone service in their town during World War I.

technique was the same that AT&T had used with its Eiffel Tower experiment, only now the proper equipment was available and it could be found in almost every country.

Sound quality of international telephone calls was not very good. Callers heard lots of buzzing and static since these calls were beamed on radio frequencies, which are subject to much interference from weather and other conditions. Nevertheless, the telephone was finally making that first, crucial step toward establishing a worldwide network.

A New Global Network

The year 1929 saw the start of a worldwide economic depression. The Great Depression slowed the growth of the American telephone network because telephones in this country depended largely on private citizens and private

A Bell Telephone executive in the United States calls England in 1923, when transatlantic calls were beamed over radio frequencies.

go. Citizens of many countries adapted slowly to telephones. In Great Britain, for example, few telephones were installed before 1900, and not everyone appreciated them. British playwright George Bernard Shaw complained that telephones shouted the caller's private business all over the house. Some British callers were even said to have telephoned each other to announce, "Stay right there; I want to come over and talk to you." Clearly, they missed the point of having a telephone.

The numbers increased nevertheless. The 1920s saw the growth of radio networks in many countries that made possible regular commercial telephone service across the oceans by 1927. By using the powerful transmitters and receivers of radio stations at both ends, telephones in New York could be connected to London that year. The basic

Many American families were reduced to poverty by the Great Depression and this slowed the telephone industry's growth. The slowdown was only temporary, however.

enterprise. Both were financially crippled by the Depression. American Bell kept installing new telephones, but the rate of growth during the 1930s was much slower than it had been during the Roaring Twenties.

Despite the slowdown in the American telephone industry, telephone networks continued to grow in other countries. This happened because in most other countries the telephone industry was owned by the national government, not private enterprise. The governments of those countries could order the construction and installation of more central exchanges, more telephones, and more radio stations. Those governments could pay for them with tax money or simply by printing more currency. Foreign governments could do this whether private industry in their countries was profitable or not.

As each country's telephone system and radio network caught up to those of the United States, more and more countries could be connected to the global telephone network, which combined radio and telephone technologies. Radio telephone service was established from the United States to nearly every country in western Europe.

By 1932 even the less-rich and less-powerful countries were tied into the global network. Starting that year, the American telephone system gained access to telephones in South Africa, Thailand, Egypt, Peru, Portugal, the Bahamas, Venezuela, and Colombia. In these countries, however, telephones were largely owned and operated by the government and military establishments. Nobody else could afford them. Typically, these countries might have one phone for every five hundred people. In some nations the ratio was even smaller.

To demonstrate that a new, truly global network had arrived, two Bell executives staged the first around-the-world telephone call in 1935. One Bell executive placed a call in New York City that was beamed across the Atlantic

Ocean by radio to another country. From there the electrical impulses hop-scotched by radio to other countries around the world, finally returning across the Pacific Ocean to another American city. The call was picked up by the AT&T long-distance network, which sent it to its intended destination: the office of another Bell executive in the very same New York office building.

When the telephone rang and the second Bell official picked up the receiver, he had a conversation that was literally an around-the-world telephone call. The words each participant heard, now lost to history, had traveled twenty-four thousand miles by radio telephone.

This call showed that the telephone network did not simply connect many countries; a single telephone message had the power to actually reach around the globe. In theory it meant that the entire world was now connected by telephone.

A New Kind of Power

The growing ability of the telephone to reach around the world gave average people a feeling of individual power as the 1930s came to a close. Most world events of the time made people feel the planet was spinning dangerously out of control. Banks were failing; people were losing their jobs, homes, and farms; bad weather ruined years of farm crops; and wars raged in Spain, Ethiopia, and the Far East.

The telephone was one thing the average person could control, even using it to reach across the troubled planet. One harmless crank from Ohio, named

As telephones spread worldwide, more and more were manufactured to meet the demand. Neatly arranged and awaiting delivery, these telephones were part of the stock of the Chesapeake & Potomac Telephone Company.

Abe Pickens, was said to have called Adolf Hitler in 1939. Apparently Pickens suggested to Hitler that the fighting should stop in Spain so that elections could take place. The story goes that when Hitler heard a voice speaking English, which he did not understand, he handed the telephone to an aide.

Even if it did occur, Pickens's call would have accomplished nothing concrete. The story did show that the global telephone network had the ability to put an average person in direct contact with an aspiring world dictator on the other side of the planet. The call was symbolic of a coming age in which mass communications would help people choose their own destinies.

The telephone had been important in running governments since World War I. With the establishment of a global network of instant communication, the telephone now became a diplomatic and key link between nations. On September 1, 1939, President Franklin D. Roosevelt was awakened by a ringing telephone beside his bed at 2:40 A.M. An American diplomat informed the president that German troops had moved deep into Poland. The next long-feared world war had begun.

"Well, Bill, it's come at last," President Roosevelt said to his caller. "God help us all."

On December 7, 1941, the Japanese air force attacked the American naval base at Pearl Harbor, Hawaii. The United States declared war on Japan the next day, and on Germany a few days later. Over the next few weeks Americans made four times more long-distance calls than during any previous period. Long-distance calling lessened slightly after that, but it remained permanently doubled by the war. Average

U.S. president Franklin D. Roosevelt signs a declaration of war against Japan on December 8, 1941. Overseas phone calls increased fourfold for a few weeks afterward.

people called each other to pass on news of friends and relatives. As wartime production sped up, businessmen made more calls to find out market news or make deals.

Wartime Demand

Despite this greatly increased telephone usage, the number of telephones, exchanges, and operators serving American civilians did not rise during the war. Instead, almost all new equipment and technicians were devoted to war work. Telephone communication was considered vital to the war effort. Military and government leaders of many nations had to be in constant telephone contact with each other to keep informed about battles and diplomatic events. A few months after the attack on Pearl Harbor, installation of new telephones in America was rationed to essential uses, which meant government and military, or industries helping with the war effort.

During World War II the number of telephones in America grew more than 30 percent, from seventeen million to twenty-two million. Most of the new telephones belonged to the government. Telephones were installed in every new American training camp and military base across the country. They were installed in every new military base around the world, too—from Europe to the Pacific islands.

The fast-growing level of demand for telephone service by both civilians and the military created a strain on telephone lines, operators, and exchanges. Callers heard more busy signals, and they had to wait several minutes for operators to make long-distance connections. By 1944 Bell officials were asking civilians to limit their telephone calls to five minutes and to keep all lines clear between 7 P.M. and 10 P.M. so that important government calls could go through. Most citizens eagerly cooperated.

Growing Pains

The war created greater need for international communications since each country needed instant information about events all over the world. AT&T and the American government worked

Smoke and flames billow from a bombed naval airfield during the Japanese attack on Pearl Harbor. The attack forced the United States into World War II and prompted AT&T to expand services worldwide.

together to speed the expansion of the global telephone network. The army laid cable that helped AT&T link American telephones to the Territory of Alaska in 1942. Radio telephone service even linked the United States to its new ally, the Soviet Union, in 1943. When the war finally ended in 1945, Americans could call almost every industrialized country on the planet by telephone. They could even call lonely military outposts in countries that had no modern industry at all.

The global telephone network did not work perfectly in those early years. Many nations in the network still had very few telephones. Also, in many foreign countries the telephone support services were poor or inadequate. An American caller often had to wait a long time for the operator to reach an overseas number. Then the result might have been a terrible connection, a wrong connection, or no connection at all.

These growing pains posed the greatest postwar challenge for the global telephone system. Scientists and

A long-distance switchboard keeps operators busy connecting calls. Switchboards were so overloaded during World War II that people were asked to limit their calls.

American soldiers staff a navy communications post in France during World War II. The soldier at left awaits commands over his radiotelephone.

By the end of World War II, telephones linked nations on all parts of the globe. This switchboard connected New York to Berne, Switzerland, in 1948.

business and government leaders were eager to solve the problems. Average American citizens were equally eager to use even more telephones in more ways in their daily lives. When peace came in 1945, the waiting list for new civilian telephones in America had over two million names on it. As the postwar era began, the United States was once again preparing to lead the world in using telephones to bring people, organizations, and countries even closer together. A new day of super mass communication was about to dawn.

CHAPTER **6**

The Mass Communications Era Dawns

The three decades after World War II became the era of super mass communications. During this period the American telephone system achieved the dream of its founders: almost everybody in America—old and young, rich and poor, urban and rural—acquired at least one telephone.

During this phase of incredibly rapid growth the biggest problem faced by the telephone company was dealing with its own success. So many people, owning so many telephones and making so many calls, led to dizzying achievements—and to near disasters. Only the steady invention and application of new technologies and systems enabled the global telephone network to pass successfully through its growing pains.

Although World War II greatly increased the number of government and military telephones in the system, wartime rationing had prevented Americans from buying many consumer items, including new telephones. During that time Americans had saved lots of money. When peace came the government took many controls off the economy, and Americans were ready and eager to spend their savings. As a result, many industries experienced a boom, or period of fast growth. Houses and cars were built by the millions for servicemen returning home from the

During the economic boom that followed World War II, Americans eagerly spent their wartime savings on cars, houses, and telephones.

war. Almost all of those new home owners wanted—and could now afford—telephones.

One reason telephones were so affordable in the 1940s and 1950s was that a government commission had frozen telephone service rates during the war. After the war the commission still had the power to regulate telephone rates, and it kept prices low. By 1948 some thirty million Bell telephones were in operation, and the number of new installations matched or broke the previous record nearly every year thereafter.

The increasing demand on the telephone system strained the central exchange offices, telephone lines, and operators. The system was facing the same problem that the telegraph had faced seventy years earlier: too many messages and not enough capacity.

The telephone company's eventual solution to this problem was to upgrade from mechanical switching of calls to electronic switching. Electronic switching can handle thousands more calls on fewer lines, with less electrical power and even less human supervision.

Transistors Revolutionize the Telephone

The invention that made all this possible was the transistor. Scientists in the Bell Research Labs invented the transistor in December 1947. Like the vacuum tube before it, the transistor is a device through which electricity flows freely. Transistors are much smaller than vacuum tubes and require far less power. They also permit much more precision in the control of electrical current. This means that electricity can be manipu-

An early transistor. The transistor improved the efficiency and power of telephone equipment and heralded the beginning of the electronics revolution.

lated to do more complex tasks. For these reasons, the transistor came to be known as the building block of modern electronics.

At first the physicists who invented the transistor—William Shockley, Walter Brattain, and John Bardeen—did not realize how versatile their invention was, nor how it would transform modern industry. The three men thought the transistor would help make better radios. As it turned out, the transistor made vastly improved, yet cheaper, radios. It also opened the way for the creation of small, powerful hearing aids, communications satellites, and computers.

For the telephone industry, the transistor meant much more efficient and powerful equipment. For consumers it meant cheaper, better, and

THE TRANSISTOR

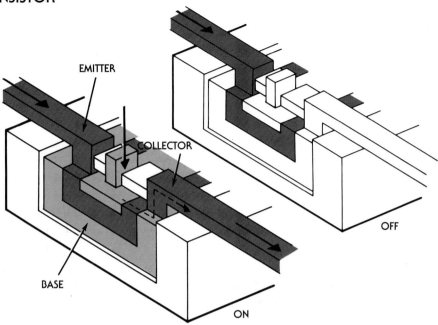

EMITTER

COLLECTOR

OFF

BASE

ON

The transistor is a tiny electronic amplifying device that revolutionized the telecommunications industry. Its high-speed capabilities enabled telephone networks to switch calls electronically.

A basic transistor acts as a switch to convey "on" or "off" electrical signals. A transistor signals "on" when an electric circuit is completed. This occurs when the base of the transistor receives a positive charge, allowing electric current to pass from the emitter to the collector. When the positive charge is removed, the circuit is broken or "off."

In a telephone network, the transistor's most important features are its small size and its ability to operate in a millionth of a second or less.

more reliable telephone service. In 1956 Shockley, Brattain, and Bardeen jointly received the Nobel Prize in physics for their massive achievement.

The only trouble was that using transistors to create electronic switching required a lot more work and experimentation than originally expected. The technology was so new and revolutionary that, like the telephone itself, it needed to be developed and tested through several generations. Only then could the communications industry af-

ford to build enough electronic switching stations to revolutionize the telephone system. Bell Labs worked on the problem all through the 1950s, but the first electronic switching station did not actually start to operate until 1965.

Microwave Relays

Meanwhile the 1950s brought many other technical improvements to the telephone system, and these improve-

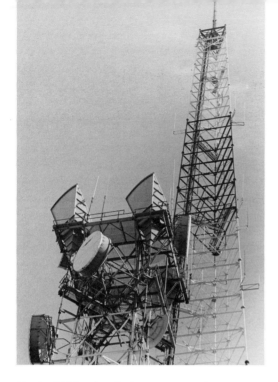

In the 1950s, the telephone company began using microwave towers to relay telephone calls across the country.

type of telephone line called coaxial cable. This is one large cable consisting of two or more smaller cables separated by insulation. Coaxial cables are capable of transmitting much more electronic information than regular copper cables, and with much less interference.

Using microwave relays and coaxial cables, customers could call anywhere in the country and it would cost less than before. AT&T passed on the savings to their customers, who in turn made even more long-distance calls. Microwave transmission also allowed some customers to begin dialing long distance directly—getting through to the desired party by themselves, without operator assistance.

Another advance over the original overseas radio telephone network came in 1956, when a transatlantic cable using transistor-powered repeaters was

Once this twenty-three-mile length of cable was laid on the ocean floor, it completed a direct telephone link between the United States and Great Britain.

ments contributed to the era of super mass communications. Radio telephoning, previously used only for international calls, was adapted to coast-to-coast calling as well. For this purpose, the telephone industry used electromagnetic waves shorter than one centimeter, called microwaves. This special kind of radio wave is very powerful and can carry many conversations, with the result that the telephone company spends less money per call.

Microwaves do not bounce over and around obstacles like regular radio waves. They can be sent only in a direct line from a sending station to a receiver. So AT&T built a series of microwave relay stations to beam nationwide telephone conversations from point to point.

To handle all the additional telephone calls once they arrived at the exchange, AT&T also constructed a new

Workers on a cable-laying ship prepare a repeater for insertion into transatlantic telephone cable in 1964.

laid on the ocean floor. The old vacuum tube repeaters had not been powerful or reliable enough for deep-water, transoceanic use. Transistor-powered repeaters could boost the power of the original caller's electronic signal dozens of times. This enabled underwater

A string of balloons marks a 5,300-mile-long undersea telephone cable being laid between Hawaii and Japan in 1964.

transatlantic message transmission. Within weeks after the cable became operational, overseas telephone traffic from America to Great Britain doubled.

Overseas calls by cable were less static filled than calls made by radio telephone. After the undersea cable to Britain proved its success, Bell soon laid similar cables to France, Germany, Alaska, and Hawaii. Clearly, the global network had overcome many of its growing pains.

New Style, New Efficiency

To make telephones even more appealing to the public, in the mid-1950s Bell began offering alternatives to the heavy, black, clumsy telephones that it had been manufacturing for decades. Customers had a choice of colors; they could select telephones that matched the decor in their offices, living rooms,

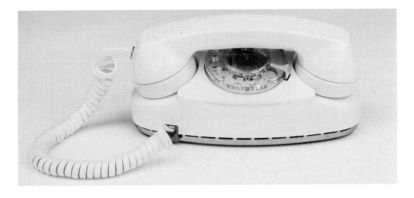

The Princess telephone introduced in 1959 was trim, lightweight, and came in pastel colors. It was one of the first alternatives to the standard, heavy, black telephone.

or bedrooms. Among the new styles was the Princess, which appeared in 1959. It was a lightweight, pastel-colored telephone, aimed at the young female buyer.

AT&T had even more sophisticated machines in mind for the 1950s. By the beginning of this decade, over sixty-six million telephones were operating in America. Overseas telephone traffic was growing so fast that all the radio frequencies, microwave channels, and undersea cables in the world would soon be unable to keep up. With some engineering data provided by Bell Labs, the United States began launching military satellites in the late 1950s. Now, the telephone company wanted to make use of the invention it had helped create.

AT&T wished to launch its own communications satellites to create even more channels for more telephones.

At AT&T's request, and funded by AT&T's money, the National Aeronautics and Space Administration (NASA) launched *Echo I* in 1960. *Echo I* was nothing more than a giant silver balloon filled with air, which orbited high in the earth's atmosphere. It contained no electronic equipment and could not electronically transmit anything at all. Instead, *Echo I* operated like a giant mirror. Its metallic skin simply bounced, or reflected microwave telephone transmissions from an earth-based sending station to an earth-based receiving station. It was a good first step.

NASA scientists prepare the first telecommunications satellite, Echo I, *launched in 1960. A simple metallic balloon,* Echo I *reflected microwave signals from one ground station to another.*

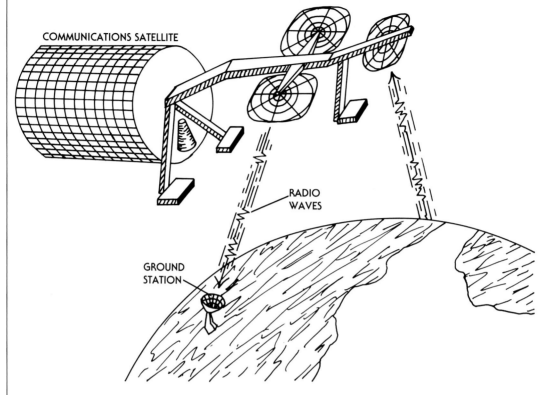

COMMUNICATIONS SATELLITES

COMMUNICATIONS SATELLITE

RADIO WAVES

GROUND STATION

Communications satellites enable thousands of telephone calls to be made at once to almost anywhere in the world. These orbiting satellites receive and transmit telephone calls via radio waves. The radio waves are beamed to a satellite from a transmitting station on earth. Once the satellite receives these radio waves, it strengthens and retransmits them to another earth station, which then connects the call. Without satellites, extensive networks of wires or cables would be needed to connect the telephones of the world.

A Highway in the Sky

AT&T's ultimate goal, though, was to launch orbiting microwave relay stations. The day President John F. Kennedy was inaugurated in 1961, AT&T received permission to launch an active, two-way communications satellite. In 1962 NASA launched *TelStar 1*, the world's first such satellite. Equipped with over one thousand transistors, *Tel-*

Star 1 acted as a giant microwave relay station in the sky, receiving thousands of transmissions and retransmitting them electronically to their destinations all over the world.

A few months after *TelStar 1*'s successful test, Congress passed a new law creating a public-private partnership company called Comsat, which would create and control all American communications satellites. From then on,

Launched in 1962, AT&T's TelStar I *was the first communications satellite able to receive, amplify, and retransmit microwave signals.*

as the worldwide public could possibly need or want.

Commercial telephone service, using Comsat satellites, began between the United States and Europe in 1965. Thanks to satellites, it became less likely than ever before that an overseas caller would have to ask for operator assistance or wait for an open line or for a connection to be made. Even around-the-world calls became fast and convenient.

Improving Telephone Transmission

the "new frontier" of space, as President Kennedy called it, opened a highway in the sky for telecommunications. Using satellites, AT&T could offer as many telephone conversations to as many telephones, and in as many countries,

Two more technological innovations were introduced in 1962 and 1963. The first, in 1962, was digital transmission. Instead of sending a very complex electrical copy of the human voice itself over a long-distance line, this system uses computers to translate the copy into a very simple two-number code, called a binary code. A computer sends this binary code to a similar computer at the

Communications satellites are often put into orbit by NASA space shuttles.

receiving exchange. The receiving computer retranslates the code back into the complex electrical copy of a voice. These impulses flow over the telephone lines to the destination telephone. The result is that a perfect copy of the original voice is heard, with absolutely no interference from the long-distance line.

The second innovation, in 1963, was the introduction by Bell of push-button dialing. This new technology made telephones even easier to use. A keypad of numbers replaced the old rotary dialer. It was faster and sleeker and seemed more in tune with the times. Computers recognized the tones made by each button and translated these tones back into numbers at the central exchange or regional telephone offices. Then the old automatic mechanical switching systems placed the call.

Electronic switching systems, using the transistors that had been invented nearly twenty years earlier, finally began to operate in 1965. Again, machines made it possible for more calls to be placed and for all calls to go through

faster. Electronic switching stations can handle 200,000 calls an hour, compared to fewer than 10,000 calls an hour, which was the capacity of earlier mechanical switching stations.

This new system began operating just in time. By the late 1960s America experienced another leap in demand for telephone service. In 1967 the number of telephones in the United States reached 100 million—one telephone for every two people in the nation. No other country has ever had anywhere near that ratio of telephones to population. In practical terms, 100 million telephones meant that virtually every household, office, and street corner in America had at least one telephone, and probably more than one. The system had tripled in size in under twenty years.

Several factors caused this increased demand. Economists called the 1960s the "go-go years." It was a time of growth and prosperity, when every person and company seemed to be making more money. The number of business calls shot up as average Americans,

Computers and push-button telephones work together to speed telephone connections.

A telephone technician works on an electronic switching system. Systems such as this one rely on fiber optics, microcomputers, and digital processing for handling large numbers of calls.

more prosperous than ever, began investing in the stock market. Personal calls also increased, as did the number of telephones in the system.

Use of the telephone system grew so quickly that, by the end of the 1960s, the service support system began breaking down, especially in big cities like New York. Sometimes a caller had to wait a few minutes for a dial tone. After getting the tone and dialing a number, the caller might have heard a busy signal even if the desired number was not really busy. Or, there might have been just a dead line—silence—no ring, no busy signal, no operator . . . nothing.

Electronic Switching

Many of the old problems that had plagued the early telephones returned in new forms. Instead of electrical interference from trolley cars, callers suffered from cross talk, two or more conversations on the same line. Sometimes both parties could hear each other; other times one set of talkers involuntar-

ily eavesdropped on the second conversation. Instead of the ghostly hisses and howls of the early 1900s, the telephone "ghosts" of the late 1960s took the form of phantom rings that signalled nothing, nobody calling. Perhaps worst of all, many people were accidentally charged for calls somebody else had made.

Electronic switching helped solve some of these problems by increasing the capacity of the system to handle many more calls much faster. Yet transistor technology alone was not always enough to prevent disasters. By 1970 only two million telephones were served by electronic switching. Sometimes even electronic switchboards could be overloaded with too many calls. When this happened, the entire system suffered a blackout, or loss of service. Every line went dead and stayed dead for hours, and sometimes even days. This happened in large sectors of major cities like New York, Boston, Denver, and Houston.

These problems tapered off as hundreds more electronic switching stations entered operation by 1975. Also,

AT&T and Bell finally built more exchanges, added new lines, and hired more operators. Outside of the largest cities, few callers probably realized there was a problem. Even in big cities, the average caller knew only that service gradually returned to normal, not that electronic switching and other improvements had begun. Callers experienced instant dial tones, rapid connections, high-quality sound transmissions, no cross talk, no ghost rings, and no mistaken charges on their bills.

In addition, electronic switching allowed many calls to go through a second or two faster. Electronic switching permitted such nice extras as three-party calls, in which three telephones may be connected temporarily for conversation on a single circuit. The most important benefit of electronic switching, however, was continued high-quality service. Without this new technology, the entire national telephone system could have broken down by the mid-1970s under the burden of skyrocketing system usage.

A total breakdown would have been disastrous. After all, many thousands of banks and businesses had come to rely heavily on telephone-linked computer systems. A total telephone system breakdown in New York or California alone would have cost tens of billions of dollars in disrupted banking, suspended business transactions, and a sudden vacuum in overseas trade.

Fortunately, a nationwide telephone breakdown never happened. Despite an occasional failure in some areas, the system continued to function almost flawlessly for many more years. Most callers simply never realized that electronic switching technology, digital transmission, and satellite and microwave relays had been activated. The truth, however, is that these new technologies cured many growing pains and prevented still others. As the final decades of the twentieth century began, it seemed clear that the era of super mass communications was well under way.

CHAPTER 7

A New Generation of Telephones and Service

The technological revolution of the super mass communications era happened mostly behind the scenes. The average caller rarely saw transistors, large computers, microwave relays, and communications satellites. Meanwhile, the telephone itself, and what the average person could do with it, remained largely unchanged from the late 1950s through the mid-1970s.

By the time the telephone marked its one-hundredth anniversary in 1976, two more revolutions were brewing, and both of them would affect average callers very much. The U.S. government was preparing to deregulate the telephone industry by removing many legal restrictions on the way the industry conducted business. At the same time, scientists were perfecting a new generation of miniature electronics. Both of these developments brought changes that average callers could see for themselves. Some of the changes caused chaos and confusion; other changes placed many new powers and abilities into the hands of average people.

Opening the Market

The legal revolution started first. For its entire history, AT&T had enjoyed an almost complete monopoly of the American telephone business. Inside the United States, no other company was allowed to provide long-distance telephone service, launch communications satellites, or make or attach telephones and other equipment to telephone lines. This monopoly allowed stable, steady progress in building a national, and then global, telephone network that offered good, reliable service.

Once that network was in place, however, there was no longer an overwhelming reason for a single company to dominate the telephone industry. In order to end AT&T's monopoly, the Department of Justice stepped in. It sued AT&T in 1974 in an effort to break the company's hold on the telephone industry. AT&T liked having control of the industry and argued that it should be allowed to keep its monopoly. Government lawyers argued that, under the free enterprise system, anyone with a good idea or a talent for business should be allowed to compete. In this case, that meant making telephones and providing a network for long-distance calls. For six years the lawyers fought.

Finally, in 1984, the parties reached an agreement. AT&T would be broken into eight separate parts. Seven regional companies, such as Pacific Bell, New England Bell, and others, would provide local service. One national company, AT&T, would offer long-distance service and would have to compete with other companies for providing that service. These other companies would also be allowed to manufacture and sell telephones, and operate pay telephones. Also, many kinds of companies would be allowed to use computers

By the 1970s, few businesses operated without telephones. This fueled the intense competition that followed the break-up of AT&T.

to provide information over the telephone.

The agreement ended more than a century of control of telephones by a single company. Over the years Americans had come to trust the telephone company, and many people even affectionately referred to AT&T as Ma Bell. But now Ma Bell was replaced by a flock of squawking competitors, all building their own long-distance networks and fighting for business.

Deregulation Brings Change

The cost of making a long-distance call went down as each company tried to appeal to average callers. For a few years, though, many people and businesses were confused and inconvenienced because some of the new companies could not build enough lines quickly or make their equipment work properly. In some cases, old problems reappeared, such as frequent busy signals, dead lines, wrong numbers, cross talk, and poor sound quality.

New problems arose, too. Many customers had to use lengthy, complicated code numbers to make long-distance calls. Callers could not always figure out which company's operators to talk to or how to reach them. Callers who were traveling could not always charge long-distance calls to their homes or offices. Information calls that used to be free now cost money. Many of the telephones made by new companies worked poorly, or not at all. Some of the long-distance companies even produced misleading advertisements to steal customers from each other.

Service gradually improved. Companies either made better equipment and satisfied their customers, or else they lost business and disappeared.

Another result of deregulation was that different companies began to offer new types of information services. These ranged from weather reports to recorded political opinions, astronomical information, and information about cultural events like movie schedules and museum shows. These recordings could be heard for only the price of a local telephone call.

Other services were created that earned a profit for their creators. Comedian Henny Youngman started this trend in New York in 1974 with "Dial-A-Joke." Every time somebody called to hear the joke of the day, Youngman made money.

After deregulation a new category of telephone-access information service began in 1980. Companies used 900 numbers and computer programs to charge callers anywhere from a few cents to a few dollars a minute. The first 900 number was created by ABC News to ask citizens, "Who won the Presidential debate—Jimmy Carter or Ronald Reagan? If you think it was President Carter, press 1. If you think Governor Reagan won, press 2." A computer tabulated the results and ABC News announced the results over the air. (Callers overwhelmingly said Reagan won; ten days later he was elected president in a landslide.)

Soon customers could call many different 900 numbers run by many different firms. Today callers can be charged money to hear updates on anything from sports contests to soap operas. Callers may also hear celebrities talking, financial or legal advice, stock market quotes, or even instruction and counsel from private detectives.

New technology also enabled companies to reach people's homes and offices in new ways. Some firms combined computers, tape recorders, and telephones to create machines that automatically call every possible number. Whenever a telephone answers, the computer plays a recorded sales pitch

for anything from newspapers to real estate. In the late 1980s, pay-per-view television began allowing some viewers to call a central number, punch in a code using the telephone keypad, and view the movie or music video of their choice.

Today the telephone industry remains far more complex and confusing than it was before the breakup of AT&T. Nonetheless, a large measure of free enterprise has spurred all the telephone companies to provide more services for less money. Despite occasional annoyances, the average telephone customer enjoys more choices and abilities than ever before.

Electronic Revolution

A second revolution—this one almost purely beneficial to average callers—occurred during the late 1970s and early

The invention of the integrated circuit in the late 1970s made possible affordable electronics equipment including cellular telephones, telephone answering machines, and personal paging systems.

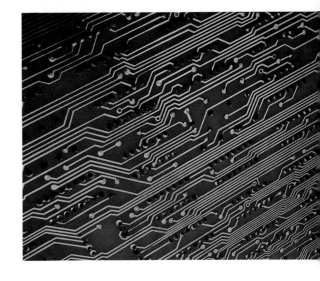

(Right) Pocket pagers are used by anyone who wants to be available by telephone on a twenty-four hour basis.

(Below) With telephone answering machines to receive and record calls, consumers miss few calls.

1980s. An invention called an integrated circuit allowed engineers to invent an affordable new generation of consumer electronic products. Among the new products were pocket pagers, answering machines, personal computers, and cellular telephones. Using these devices, people could send almost anything over the telephone lines. People could also place and receive calls to and from almost any location, whether a permanent telephone or line was there or not.

Answering machines are perhaps the simplest and most common example of how this technological revolution in consumer electronics has changed the way we use our telephones. A small but complex computer board is installed inside a small machine, which is then plugged into the telephone. The computer can be programmed to answer the telephone, play a message recorded by the owner, and record the caller's message. In this way, a person does not even have to be present to take a call.

Pocket pagers extend this idea further. They are electronic devices small enough to clip onto clothing or slip inside a purse or pocket. With the help of special radio receivers, users can be notified by microwave transmission when someone is trying to call. Most pagers vibrate or emit a beep when activated. Some also have a calculator-type computer display screen that shows the telephone number of the person who called.

At first, pocket pagers were very expensive, and they worked only in a relatively small area, such as a single city. They were used chiefly by highly paid professionals who had to be available at a moment's notice or in case of emergency. Today pocket pagers are more affordable, and they can be used by almost anyone who wants to be available by telephone on a twenty-four hour basis. The most complex paging systems can reach the user almost anywhere on the globe.

Personal computers, called PCs, also became popular in the early 1980s. Using a computer-telephone hookup called a modem, PC users could use telephone lines to transfer many kinds of information from one computer to another. Among the things that can be transmitted are photographs, copies of documents, banking records, medical diagnostics, newspaper and magazine articles, and even entire books.

Modem-equipped PCs enabled average people to perform many tasks quickly by computer over the telephone. These tasks once required a physical trip to an office, or at least a telephone conversation with a business representative. These activities include banking, airline ticket reservations and purchases, and even buying groceries.

Some people began using modems and PCs to work at home and send their work, including everything from the written word to diagrams, drawings, and plans, back to a main office in another town or even another state. This process is called telecommuting. It has been estimated that one million workers were at least part-time telecommuters by the early 1990s.

Modems may also be used to com-

By connecting to a telephone, computers can transmit photographs, banking records, and other documents quickly and over long distances.

thing from poetry to baseball. In the early 1990s modems even began to send moving video pictures and graphics-oriented video games from one person's PC or video game console to another.

A Global Phone Booth

Cellular telephones became popular in the mid-1980s. These are small, portable, wireless telephones that include short-range radio receivers and transmitters. Using antennas like those on portable radios, cellular telephones give callers physical freedom and mobility. People are no longer tied by short cords to their telephone jacks. Instead, for example, they can walk around their yards and water the grass while talking or making calls. Cellular telephones in automobiles allow callers to converse while driving, even if they are on remote highways, dozens of miles from the nearest town or city. Airlines now offer cellular telephone service for anyone who needs to make calls during a flight.

World economic markets rise and fall with information exchanged through telecommunications equipment like that found at the New York Stock Exchange.

municate by telephone in the other direction—from a central office to a remote location. This allows businesspeople to monitor and control machines by telephone. Types of machines that are monitored in this way range from automatic bank tellers to electronic dart games in neighborhood taverns.

Modems also allow live, two-way communication with other PC users by central computer data banks called electronic bulletin boards (EBB). Callers can also post electronic messages for other bulletin board users to read later. Dozens of EBBs have been created for special-interest groups, allowing users to read or write messages about every-

The cellular telephone adds mobility to an already mobile society.

Businesspeople can stay in touch with their offices even when a stationary telephone is nowhere nearby.

The latest cellular telephones are so small (a few inches long), so light (under half a pound), and so powerful that people are using them in restaurants, department stores, bleachers at sports stadiums, golf courses, and even public restrooms.

Like most new technologies, cellular telephones bring both advantages and disadvantages. Many users enjoy their flexible communication ability. People waiting for important calls no longer have to be prisoners, waiting by their telephones. Commuters can turn wasted flying or driving time into productive or enjoyable conversation. Callers can notify police or traffic control authorities about crimes and emergencies in progress.

Not everyone enjoys being surrounded by constant beeps, rings, and one-sided conversations, however. These can be especially annoying in public places that are supposed to be quiet, like movie theaters and museums. Also, police note that criminals who use cellular telephones are even harder to find and catch. Some people wonder whether it is really such a good thing to be in touch with everyone at all times.

People have thought about this issue ever since the telephone itself was invented, but the point today is that cellular telephones have taken down another barrier between public and private space. As one magazine reporter wrote, everyone who owns and uses a cellular telephone is "now living in a global phone booth."

Fax by Phone

Fax machines are the latest telephone-related consumer product to achieve worldwide popularity. ("Fax" is short for "facsimile," or exact copy.) Beginning in the late 1980s, computer technology became so powerful and affordable that people could use fax machines to send photocopies over the telephone. While PCs and modems allow the transfer of data from one computer to another, fax machines can send physical copies of any piece of paper anywhere in the world, almost instantly.

Today faxes are used worldwide to send legal documents, press releases,

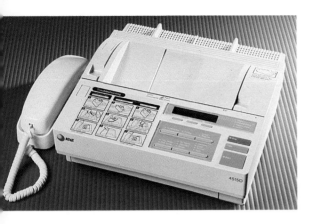

Facsimile, or fax, machines can send photocopies of documents anywhere in the world via telephone transmission.

medical information, drawings, pictures, photographs, and more. Every day faxes help people close business deals or learn important details of legal and political situations. Faxes can help catch suspects, as when police send photographs of wanted criminals over the line.

Faxes can even help save lives. A current television commercial demonstrates this with a dramatic scene that may someday become routine. The advertisement shows a doctor working on a young patient in a hospital emergency room. The physician turns to a nurse and says, "Fax a permission form to his parents, so we can operate!" When the signed permission comes back by fax after a few moments, the doctor prepares to perform the needed surgery.

Faxes have also been used by political resistance movements to fight against tyranny. When China's government killed protesters with tanks in 1989, Chinese students around the world used fax machines and telephone lines to keep Chinese citizens and the world informed of what was happening. In 1989 and 1990 Kuwaitis used faxes to tell the world about the occupation of their country by invaders from Iraq. During the attempted coup against Soviet president Mikhail Gorbachev in 1991, Soviet citizens used privately owned fax machines and international telephone lines to tell the world about the attempted takeover. In each case, average people were able to use telephones and modern technology to help shape world opinion and even to help affect the course of world history.

As the world began the countdown to the twenty-first century, the average caller could do much more with a telephone than Alexander Graham Bell ever imagined would be possible. A wide-open, free-market system, combined with an ongoing revolution in technology, has allowed the world to go far beyond using telephones for voice communication only.

Today people and machines communicate in many ways by means of the telephone. Over telephone lines around the world, people send live and recorded voices, electronic data, music, and moving pictures. Today's telephone, assisted by the computer, TV, and other devices, has helped create an environment in which many people can hear the same electronic drumbeat all over the planet and can even add their own individual rhythms to the worldwide telephonic symphony.

No wonder Alfred Sikes, chairman of the U.S. Federal Communications Commission, said in 1991: "We're at a seminal [turning] point. We are moving from the Age of Information to an Age of Knowledge."

Telephones of the Future

Tomorrow's telephones will not be instruments just for talking and listening. They will also enable people to send and receive all kinds of information, including sounds, pictures, diagrams, computer data bases, computer simulations, movies on demand, and every other form of electronic data. Low-orbiting satellites, combined with cellular telephone technology, will make it possible to place and receive calls from anywhere on earth. "Vast new capacity will push down prices so that casual chats will be as routine across the ocean as they are across town," reported one business magazine.

At the same time, telephones will continue to become ever-smaller, lighter, and easier to use. Eventually the visible parts of a telephone may disappear. Instead of a small box with buttons and a handset, a telephone might someday be replaced by tiny computers hidden in people's clothing, cars, offices, or houses. Twenty-five years from now a caller who wants to use a telephone may speak a command aloud, causing a projection of light to float in the air. This projection could look like a three-dimensional television screen and function like a computer. Elements of such a system are already in the early stages of development in scientific laboratories.

The Secret of Tomorrow

Many simpler changes in telephone technology are currently under way in today's marketplace. Motorola, Qualcomm, and the Loral Corporation have

A 1980s model telephone with a built-in switchboard is a harbinger of even more dramatic changes to come.

Advanced technology has made it possible to combine a telephone and an answering machine into one instrument.

announced plans to launch fleets of orbiting satellites that will pick up and retransmit cellular telephone calls anywhere in the world. Service is scheduled to begin in 1997.

Today's telephones are constantly shrinking in size. As one Motorola executive said, "The secret of the phone [of tomorrow] is in miniaturizing components like the battery, antenna, and fil-

ters, and packing them more densely within the phone itself." At the same time, telephones are gaining new features and becoming easier to use. "The phone of the future will be feature-oriented [able to do many more things than just receive and transmit voices]," said an official at Northern Telecom. "It will have a screen and be able to draw from the [computer] network system." The Northern Telecom spokesman added, "We want to make it a 'no brainer,' to make the telephone easy to operate. That's going to be necessary for all of these services we see coming."

Services that will be built into tomorrow's telephone include features that in the early 1990s required a separate machine, such as a computer, answering machine, caller identification device, and central switchboard. Future telephones will include built-in voice mail, a service that takes messages. Tomorrow's telephones will perform call-screening functions, letting users hear the voices of callers before responding to incoming calls. Tomorrow's tele-

As telephones become smaller and smaller they also become more mobile and more efficient.

A single-unit, full-color videophone transmits real images much like those seen on television. Telephones such as this enable distant family and friends to converse and see each other without leaving home.

phones will have caller identification programs that display on a small screen the name and telephone number of origin for an incoming call. One cordless telephone recently developed by the Jerrold Cable TV Company also functions as a hand-held television remote-control device.

Video Telephones

Most dramatically, telephones of the future will have video screens to allow live, two-way pictures. With this feature the caller and the called party will be able to see each other during conversation. Built-in video screens will also enable users to send, receive, and see graphics, photographs, and moving images from personal and public film and video libraries.

Today video telephones are available only under certain circumstances. Users must pay a lot of money to send

and receive live video phone calls. Sometimes users must place outgoing video calls from special studios where equipment is on hand and where video

In fiber-optic cable, long, hairlike strands of glass carry telephone messages by laser light.

Pinpoints of light emerge from fiber-optic glass strands (left). Ribbonlike components (below) shelter hair-thin, ultrapure glass fiber light guides used to speed the exchange of information worldwide.

transmission is easy. Most of the time to-day's video telephone calls send pictures only one way. Only voices go back to the call's origination point.

Finally, the quality of most video transmissions is not very good today. The old coaxial cables, electronic switching stations, transmission gear, and computer software simply are not powerful enough to carry high-quality video images. Video telephone transmissions will not become widespread, inexpensive, and visually flawless until a new kind of cable, called fiber-optic cable, is installed across the country and around the world.

Fiber-optic cable was invented in 1970. It is made of individual glass lines no thicker than a hair, all wound to-

FIBER-OPTIC COMMUNICATIONS

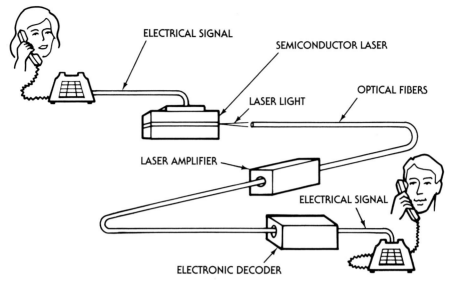

Telephone systems in many countries are converting to fiber-optic cables. Japan is closest to achieving this goal while only 6 percent of the American telephone network is linked by fiber-optic cables.

Fiber-optic communications systems use light instead of electricity to carry telephone signals. In a fiber-optic system, electrical signals from a telephone pass through a semiconductor laser. This device changes electrical signals into laser light.

Laser light can travel many miles along hair-thin strands of glass called optical fibers. Since light can carry billions of bits of information, a single optical fiber can transmit as much information as can hundreds of copper electrical wires. When the laser light reaches its destination, another semiconductor then changes, or decodes, the light signals into electrical signals used by telephones.

gether inside a single cable. Instead of sending electrical current, as the old copper cables do, fiber optics transmit high-speed flashes of laser light through the glass fibers for thousands of information channels. This light is used to send a high volume of very complex information to the destination telephone or computer.

The cost of installing fiber-optic cable, video telephones, satellite transmission systems, and advanced computerized central exchanges to work with all this equipment is very high. It will prob-

ably cost hundreds of billions of dollars. Once a fiber-optic network is in place, the cost of instantly sending vast quantities of electronic pictures and information all over the world, will be low.

At present, fiber-optic cables are used in only 6 percent of the total American telephone network. Fiber optics are mostly employed in trunk lines that connect telephone company exchange stations, and in undersea telephone cables. Of all the countries in the world, Japan is moving fastest to install a nationwide network of fiber-optic cable. The Japanese telephone industry is owned and run by the government, which has decided to have fiber-optic lines going to every Japanese home and business by the year 2015. Japan is relying chiefly on fiber-optic systems designed, built, and installed by AT&T.

In the United States, a public network of fiber optics may take longer to blanket the country. Congress and the courts began arguing in 1990 about who will control and profit from the sale of information over a fiber-optic system. It will take time to settle this argument and pass the proper laws and regulations. Only then can private companies begin building and installing fiber-optic networks and lines to every American office and household.

Meanwhile, some private companies are not waiting for the telephone industry to provide fiber optics to the public. These companies are installing and building their own fiber-optic video telephone systems. In Southern California, General Telephone & Electronics has installed a test market of some two hundred fiber-optic lines that provide services combining computer, video, and telephone technologies.

Also on a test basis, some rural hospitals are transmitting X rays by video telephone to major hospitals for expert diagnosis. By 1994 General Electric (GE) will have built its own fiber-optic telephone network, allowing GE employees around the globe to call each other by dialing just seven numbers. Every call on GE's internal network will be a face-to-face, two-way video transmission.

The growing network of communications technology around the world requires even more sophisticated operations centers.

Eventually the effect of fiber optics will be felt by every caller. In the year 2010 the main telephone in most houses might resemble a combination of a big-screen television, a computer, and drafting table. A person could use it to do work and then send that work to a school or office, to see the latest movies, play games, or to see and speak with a person in another country.

By the year 2015 a telephone might resemble a pair of lightweight, plastic eyeglasses. Computerized optics and miniaturized speakers would be embedded in the glasses. They would let a caller see and hear a scene transmitted from another telephone.

Some future telephones might not have any visible parts at all. Instead, there might be a special place where a caller stands or sits. Using voice-recognition technology, already in use in the early 1990s, the caller's voice command would open a telephone channel. Live, three-dimensional pictures of the called party could be projected in midair, using a video monitor and special curved mirrors hidden in the floor, walls, or furniture.

Clearly the telephone is on the verge of an exciting new era of development. Changes are already occurring that will affect the telephone instrument itself, the services and functions it provides and performs, the support services it uses, and the daily lives of people all over the planet who use this technology. The telephone will continue to change faster and faster as science advances.

The effect of tomorrow's powerful telephone and computer networks on society will be far-reaching. Experts have long described modern civilization as a "global village." Once every person can call every other person on the planet for a casual chat, quickly, easily and affordably, then the global village will truly be a reality. Government, diplomacy, science, medicine, education, and business will achieve a breathtaking efficiency and will create a powerful new blending of knowledge and effort. Finally, the growing, instant availability of all forms of art, entertainment, and information by telephone and computer will continue to shift the base of our culture from the print media to the electronic media.

Telephones will continue to support and channel electronic data of every kind, from every source, to and from every point on earth. However great the changes, telephones will remain the central nervous system for the ongoing electronic communications revolution.

Glossary

■■

battery: A storage device that can hold and supply electric current.

cable: A set of insulated wires for carrying telephone or telegraph messages.

carbon button: A telephone part that contains small grains of the element known as carbon. When electricity flows strongly or weakly through this "button," the carbon grains pack together or spread apart in response. The movement of the grains makes the button vibrate in such a way that it re-creates the sound of a human voice.

cellular telephone: A portable radio telephone that does not need to be plugged into a telephone line.

central exchange: An office run by the telephone company, where the caller's telephone line is connected to the line of the person whom the caller wants to reach.

circuit: A closed path for electrical current, especially one connecting two telephones. Also, any device with conductors, vacuum tubes, and other parts through which current passes.

coaxial cable: An electrical transmission line in which there are two concentric (one inside the other) conductors separated by insulation.

communications satellite: A satellite equipped to receive and transmit microwave signals.

conductor: A substance that moves electricity along or through some other substance, such as metal wire.

connection: A completed circuit or successful telephone transmission.

contact: The part of a circuit that touches or moves away from the wire to complete or break an electric circuit.

cross talk: Two or more conversations accidentally transmitted on the same telephone line.

current: Steady impulses of electricity.

deregulation: Removing laws, rules, and restrictions that used to control an industry.

diaphragm: The thin, vibrating part of a telephone that reproduces sounds. Today it is contained inside the earpiece.

digital transmission: Using computers to translate sounds into simple two-number codes. At the receiving end, another computer retranslates the code into sounds.

electromagnet: An iron bar that becomes magnetic when an electrified wire is wrapped around it.

electronics: The development and use of advanced electrical devices, such as vacuum tubes and transistors.

electronic switching: Transistor-powered devices for transferring calls from the caller's telephone to the destination telephone.

fax: Short for "facsimile." A physical copy of a picture or document that is copied electronically and sent by telephone transmission.

fiber optics: A technology for telephone lines using thin, hairlike lines of very pure glass. Lasers send light through these lines instead of sending electricity, as in older telephone and telegraph systems.

frequency: Speed or rate of vibration.

ground: A contact complete to earth, or some safe place, that enables electricity to complete a circuit, so that users of equipment do not receive an electric shock.

harmonic telegraph: A device for sending many messages at the same time over a single telegraph wire. It uses different rates of vibration in the sending and receiving instruments for each message sent, thus creating different electrical impulses.

insulation: The wrapping around an electric wire to prevent interference.

interference: The fading of electric or radio impulses or signals because of static or unwanted signals.

line: A wire used to transmit telephone or telegraph messages.

loading coil: A relay battery placed every mile or so along telephone wires. It greatly improved the quality of long-

distance calling in the early 1900s.

magneto: A small generator that uses permanent magnets for creating electric current.

microwave: Short electromagnetic wave.

modem: A device that allows a computer to transmit electronic data over telephone wires.

monopoly: The control of all business in a certain geographic area or in a certain industry.

Morse code: A system invented by Samuel Morse that uses long and short dashes, sounds, or flashes of light to symbolize each letter of the alphabet.

operator: A professional technician who works at a telephone switchboard or telegraph key.

patent: The legal right to be sole owner of an idea or creation.

picture phone: A video telephone connected to a private circuit, capable of sending and receiving both live voices and video images of the caller and the called party.

radio telephone: An instrument that transmits long-distance calls by radio waves.

receiver: The handset or earpiece of a telephone. Also, any device that receives electrical transmissions.

relay: An electrical relay is a battery

located on an electrified wire, between the sending and destination points. The relay adds fresh electrical power to help the current go farther along the line.

repeaters: An advanced type of relay that actually rebuilds and retransmits the electrical patterns.

resistance: Forces that prevent electricity from moving with all possible speed and power.

semaphore: A visual code that represents each letter of the alphabet by changing the position of two arms, sticks, or flags.

telecommunications: The sending and receiving of messages by telephone.

telecommuter: Someone who works at home and sends work to the office over the telephone, usually with a computer and modem.

telegraph: From the Greek, this word literally means "distant writing." An electric telegraph is a device for sending messages along an electric wire. It works by stopping and starting the flow of electricity in a controlled way that can be seen or recorded on the far end of the wire.

telephone: From the Greek, this word literally means "distant sound." A telephone makes an electric copy of a voice or other sound, sends that copy along a wire in the form of electric impulses, and retranslates the impulses into the original sounds at the far end.

transistor: A device for amplification and control of electric current.

transmission: Sending controlled electric impulses along a wire or through the airwaves.

transmitter: A device capable of performing transmission.

vacuum tube: A sealed glass tube with no air inside (a vacuum). The tube contains small electric wires and conducts electricity more efficiently than when air is present.

variable resistance: Barriers of changing strength that block or allow the flow of electricity.

vibration: Rapid movement back and forth.

For Further Reading

H.M. Boettinger, *The Telephone Book: Bell, Watson, Vail, and American Life.* Croton-on-Hudson, NY: Riverwood Publishers, 1977.

Egon Larsen, *Ideas and Invention.* London: Spring Books, 1960.

Men of Science and Invention. New York: American Heritage/Harper & Row, 1960.

Jerome Meyer, *World Book of Great Inventions.* Cleveland and New York: World Publishing, 1956.

Kathy Pelta, *Alexander Graham Bell.* Englewood Cliffs, NJ: Silver Burdett, 1989.

Katherine B. Shippen, *Mr. Bell Invents the Telephone.* New York: Random House, 1952.

Works Consulted

John Brooks, *Telephone, The First Hundred Years.* New York: Harper & Row, 1975.

Robert V. Bruce, *Bell: Alexander Graham Bell and the Conquest of Solitude.* Boston: Little, Brown, 1973.

Peter Coy, "How Do You Build an Information Highway?" *Business Week*, September 16, 1991.

Peter Coy and Michele Galen, "Let's Not Let Phone Pollution Hang Up Free Speech," *Business Week*, August 19, 1991.

Peter Coy et al., "Super Phones," *Business Week*, October 7, 1991.

Will Dunham, "900-Number Abuses Ring Alarm Bells," *Los Angeles Times*, April 21, 1991.

Paul Farhi, "Waves of the Future," *The Washington Post*, May 5, 1991.

Dan Gutman, "Long, Long Distance," *Discover*, January 1991.

Greg Johnson, "Qualcomm, Loral to Develop Satellite-Based Phone System," *Los Angeles Times*, October 11, 1991.

Gary Kim, "Telcos, Cable on Similar Paths," *Multichannel News*, June 25, 1990.

Charles Leerhsen et al., "If a Movie Usher Answers," *Business Week*, August 26, 1991.

John Lippman, "How the Line Between Cable, Phones May Blur," *Los Angeles Times*, October 16, 1991.

Martha McDonald, "Cordless Market Continues Strong," *This Week in Consumer Electronics*, November 4, 1991.

"May the Best Fiber Optics Win," *Business Week*, September 16, 1991.

Clemens P. Work, "Wiring the Global Village," *U.S. News & World Report*, February 26, 1990.

Index

About the Author

■■■

Marcus Webb is editor of *RePlay* magazine, the leading trade publication for the coin-operated amusement industry. Webb received a bachelor of arts degree in English, with honors, from the University of Virginia. He has shared speakers' platforms with Ronald Reagan and Barry Goldwater, and some of his speeches have been printed in the *Congressional Record.* He lives in Southern California with his wife, Margot, an author.

Picture Credits

■■■